The Adventures of Buffalo and Tough Cookie

Morristown Centennial Library
Regulations
(802) 888-3853
www.centenniallibrary.org
centenniallib2@yahoo.com

Unless a shorter time is indicated, books and magazines may be borrowed for four weeks, audio books on tape and CD may be borrowed for three weeks, and videos and DVDs may be borrowed for one week. All library materials may be renewed once for the same time period.

A fine of five cents a day every day open will be charged on all overdue library books and audio books. A fine of one dollar a day every day open will be charged for overdue library videos and DVDs.

No library material is to be lent out of the household of the borrower.

All damage to library materials beyond reasonable wear and all losses shall be made good by the borrower.

Library Hours

Sunday & Monday	Closed
Tuesday	9:30am – 7 pm
Wednesday	9:30am – 7pm
Thursday	10am – 5:30pm
Friday	10am – 5:30pm
Saturday	9am – 2pm

THE ADVENTURES OF

Buffalo and Tough Cookie

A Hiking Journey of Discovery Through
New Hampshire's "52 With a View" Mountain List

Dan Szczesny

BONDCLIFF BOOKS
Littleton, New Hampshire

Library of Congress Control Number: 2013939658

ISBN-10: 1-931271-30-5

ISBN-13: 978-1-931271-30-1

DISCLAIMER: Every effort was made to ensure that the information in this book was accurate at press time. However, conditions are subject to change. We would appreciate hearing of any such changes.

Design and text composition by Passumpsic Publishing, St. Johnsbury, Vermont.

Printed in the United States by Sherwin Dodge Printers, Littleton, New Hampshire

A majority of the photographs appearing in this volume were taken by the author. The exceptions are as follows:
Cover design and front cover image by Peter Noonan.
Back cover image by Meenakashi Gyawali.

Additional copies of this book may be obtained directly from:
Bondcliff Books
P.O. Box 385
Littleton, NH 03561
www.bondcliffbooks.com

TO MEENAKSHI,
my everything

AND TO AARON,
our greatest fan

CONTENTS

FOREWORD

When Dan first told me he was writing a book, I was thrilled. I'm a long-time admirer of his EKP Adventures blog—thanks to Dan, many of my afternoons have been lost in vivid dreams of Nepal and Kala Patthar—and I was very glad to know the world would soon enjoy a bound work of Mr. Szczesny's nonfiction.

The topic of this book is near and dear to my heart. Dan hikes with a young girl throughout the White Mountains, tackling peaks often overlooked by the average New England peakbagger. Together, he and this remarkable young lady, Janelle, summit all 52 mountains on a list known as the "52 With a View." The two trekkers battle severe weather, fatigue, and the occasional naysayer. I had similar experiences with my daughter, Alex, as we hiked the New Hampshire Four Thousand Footers during 2008 and 2009. I chronicled those experiences in my book, *Up: A Mother and Daughter's Peakbagging Adventure* (Broadway Books, 2012). There's a significant difference between my memoir and Dan's, however. I was hiking with my own child, someone I have obviously known since birth and someone I have personally raised since the day she was born. Dan, on the other hand, hiked with a child that was not related to him. As a result, not only did the two share outdoor adventures, but they forged a friendship that bridged the traditional gaps of age and gender. Theirs is a team not formed of traditional family ties but, instead, an earned and mutual respect. The former comes far more easily than the latter; mother-daughter bonds are a natural happenstance of parenthood, but a true friendship between an adult and a child requires far more patience, understanding, and trust. Dan and Janelle are a unique and inspiring duo.

My daughters and I have had the privilege of hiking with "Buffalo and Tough Cookie," as Dan and Janelle are called on the trails, on three occasions. Each occasion was an absolute pleasure. Alex and Sage enjoy Janelle's company; it's rare my daughters encounter such a strong and hard-core hiker so close to their own ages. When together, the three young ladies hike ahead of the adults and immerse themselves in animated discussion. They direct one another's attentions to those minute and seemingly inconsequential details we grown-ups tend to miss, and they sometimes have conversations that come to an abrupt halt when the adults draw too near. It's been a treat to watch these intrepid females take on nature while simultaneously hitting it off.

Though Tough Cookie is the star of this book, as she should be, Buffalo deserves serious credit and accolades for what he has accomplished. Hiking 52 mountains within the course of one year is difficult enough when you're on your own. Hiking 52 mountains within the course of one year with a child—an unrelated child, at that—must have been extraordinarily difficult in numerous ways. Hiking with a child means hiking with an ever-present worry about safety. It means hiking with a ton of weight on your back so you can be optimally prepared if the two of you have an emergency and need to spend the night out. It means carrying whatever is in the child's backpack if her load becomes too heavy. It means dealing with those obnoxious and ignorant naysayers, the people who swear girls can't or shouldn't hike, or who discredit a girl's ability by insisting an adult is pushing her forward. Hiking with a child means constantly monitoring someone else's pace, making sure someone else always eats enough food and drinks enough liquid, it means making sure no one overheats or gets too cold or sweats off their sunblock. It means so, so much more than it does when you hike solo or with other adults. I know what that's like, and I tip my hat to Dan in the utmost admiration and respect. In a world still unfortunately full of men who underplay or outright dismiss the chutzpah of girls, Dan took Janelle's ambitions seriously and he facilitated her success. Would more adults do the same for our next generation of young women?

It's clear I'm a fan of Buffalo and Tough Cookie. I'll wager my hiking boots you will be too. For not only is Dan an excellent writer, he's witty, kind, generous, and just plain fun to be around. Janelle, in addition to being a positive and intelligent young lady, embodies the strong female spirit all girls share but only some get the chance to express. No doubt these personal qualities will make themselves obvious to the reader as the engaging chapters are perused.

So — grab a cup of tea, find your favorite comfy chair, and experience New Hampshire's beautiful 52 With a View through the intrepid adventures of Buffalo and Tough Cookie.

Patricia Ellis Herr

FEBRUARY 2013

INTRODUCTION

A Journey of Many Miles, the Challenge of One Step

When the third police officer arrived and Janelle instinctively inched closer to me, I couldn't help wondering how I had gotten us into this mess, and how I was going to get us out.

Saturday had started off cool but clear. Following the success of our hike the weekend before to another local park at the other end of our city, Manchester, then 9-year-old Janelle and I decided to explore another city trail system, an old park called Nutts Pond. Located in a more industrialized section of the city — the strip — the pond and area around it played an important role in Manchester's history.

The pond's namesake was "Commodore" George Washington Morrison Nutt, whose family owned the pond in the late nineteenth century. Nutt was a 24-inch-tall circus performer who toured with Tom Thumb and wore a military outfit while singing to an adoring crowd.

But now, unfortunately, as Janelle and I made our way over the small bridge that led to the trail, it was clear that the pond's glory days as a swimming hole and recreational attraction were long gone.

The pond was trashed, literally. Shopping carts from nearby supermarkets littered the bottom of the pond like skeletal remains. Garbage was everywhere, in the water and in the woods along the trail. The trail was saturated with graffiti. It covered everything, from the sides of the bridge, to the remains of the concrete weir, to the park benches along the water, and to the paved trail itself. Every flat man-made surface was tagged.

I briefly considered leaving and finding another area to explore, not because I felt any physical danger, but because Nutts Pond was a joyless place. The strip of "woods" between the pond and the development to the west was only about 50 feet wide, and the only thing of any real interest was the remains of the abandoned railroad track that runs behind the pond.

The paved section of the trail was about a half mile long, before becoming a dirt path behind a variety of warehouses and businesses. Our plan for the day was to continue down the path to Goffs Falls Road, where we'd check out an old railroad old trestle, and then hike up to Barnes & Noble to await a ride back to our car from my wife, Meenakshi, who was spending the day with Janelle's brother, Aaron.

But then the police showed up and our lives changed. I should mention that Janelle is not my daughter.

IN NOVEMBER 2010, I was a newlywed. My Nepalese wife, Meenakshi, and I had just returned to New Hampshire from Nepal, at the top of our game. We had married in Kathmandu, then made a life-changing trek to Mount Everest Base Camp. Along the way we scaled 18,350-foot Kala Patthar, the highest we had ever been.

On previous expeditions, we had hiked the Centennial Trail across South Dakota, where I had earned my nickname after running scared off the trail to get out of the way of what I thought was a herd of trampling buffalo. It turned out the herd was only two babies playing. The name stuck.

We had also spent days in the bottom of the Grand Canyon, where mule deer had grazed just outside our tent and coyotes howled us to sleep at night.

We are both members of Appalachian Mountain Club's New Hampshire Four Thousand Footer Club, whereby you earn a club certificate by scaling all forty-eight our state's highest mountains.

When we returned from Nepal — married, strong, invincible — we began to search for some new adventure, the next challenging, demanding, taxing quest with which to notch our well-worn belts.

How could we have guessed that adventure would come to us in the form of 9-year-old twins named Janelle and Aaron?

THEY WERE OUR NEIGHBORS, these two. Twins by birth, but worlds apart in temperament and interests, yet always together. We knew them slightly, the two kids who lived next door. The kids who got in my way when I tried to cut the lawn. The kids who went scream-

Buffalo and Tough Cookie, along with Meg, Ian and Aaron, prepare for their first hike, up Bald Mountain in Franconia Notch State Park.

ing down the alley out back in the summer. The kids who lived not with their parents but with their grandparents, Sara and Jim.

In the spring of 2011 all our lives changed when Meena lost her job and Jim, the twins' grandfather, passed away. We came together in a terrible burst of pain and confusion, two families adrift and looking for comfort.

The twins suddenly began navigating toward us, and with Meena home that summer, I began to come home to a full house, kids running around, helping in the garden, playing in the basement, coming with me as I took trips to the market or the movies.

The twins adopted us. And we let them.

But we had no experience in such matters, no warm-up to dealing with pre-tweens. They just were there. So we went on living, and hiking, because that's what we did anyway. It seemed natural to simply take them along.

The White Mountain National Forest is a 750,000-acre swath of timber, tourists and trails in the northern part of our state. There are hundreds of mountains, and an equal amount of trails, some as challenging and terrifying as anything the Rockies could throw into a hiker's path. So that's where we took them.

That summer, it all began with a short hike up Bald Mountain, a small, family-friendly mountain in Franconia Notch State Park. We took the twins, along with my niece and nephew. The summit is open and there's plenty of rock for kids to scramble around on. After, on her own, Janelle asked me if we could do that again, hike again.

I said of course, but that we'd have to coordinate something with Meena and the rest of the kids. Looking back on that day, I still remember very clearly how she responded. She said, "That's OK, you can just take me." I should have known then there was something special happening.

SO WE STARTED HIKING, the girl and I. We began easy with city parks and neighborhood walks. We worked our way up to little hills — Rock Rimmon, a 300-foot shelf park around the corner from our houses, then the Uncanoonucs, double 1,000-footers one town over, then Pack Monadnock, a 2,200-foot beauty in the southern part of the state.

And all through it she never asked if we were there yet.

So, on Nov. 5, 2011, on an icy cold but bright blue day, we climbed to the top of 2,900-foot Mount Kearsarge, the first mountain on our list. It was just us two. At that stage she used Meenakshi's gear and her own beat-up purple coat and a bright pink princess hat.

At the summit, she threw snowballs and explored the ruins of the old watchman cabin. We sat together under the fire tower and ate peanuts and M&Ms. It was cold, but she was warm. She was tired but she never mentioned it. She just wandered around in a daze, wanted to see everything, every viewpoint, every man-made object, every rock and every hunk of ice.

Like I did my first time above treeline in New Hampshire.

We hiked another 52er in Waterville Valley next, the popular Welch-Dickey loop, where we were amazed to be confronted by mountain bikers at the summit. She stood there watching them pedal back down

Janelle is geared up and ready to tackle Pack Monadnock in bad weather.

off the steep cliff and shook her head and smiled, too joyful to attach any words to that experience.

Then, in March 2012, on a freakishly warm day, we hiked Mount Monadnock in the state's southwest corner, and the charms of this most popular of New Hampshire mountains made a believer out of her. Janelle skittered along those ledges like she was made to be there. She climbed and climbed, purposely finding the most difficult way to tackle a steep pitch or rock shelf. Monadnock sealed the deal for her. Later, we had a conversation about mountain lists. My original goal was to train her to eventually hike a 4,000-footer, the gold standard of mountains among the state's hiker community. But that was just fool's gold, for as soon as I mentioned the fact that we had climbed three mountains on the 52 With a View list, she never hesitated.

"Why don't we just finish that list?" she asked.

So that is what we set off to do, in one year's time.

I CAME TO UNDERSTAND that this list was different, and special. There were trip reports out there online, and the group of hikers who originally created the list still hiked. The Over the Hill Hikers of Sandwich built this list originally as a way for older hikers to find companionship and get exercise while hiking what were advertised as some of the state's easier peaks. Those people were full of it.

Shelburne Moriah is on the list, a 12-mile round trip in the northeast corner of the Whites that demands river crossings, steep uphills and a long exposed ridge walk.

Iron Mountain is on the list, a short hike but over a brutally eroded, root-lined trail that would tax the heartiest hiker, all to reach a viewless summit that forces the hiker to go another half mile to find a vista.

There are others. Success Mountain: a mud bog. Hayes: an impossible-to-find-and-drive access road. Magalloway: eight miles of north country logging roads to get to the trailhead. Stairs: remote and steep. What seniors could possibly think these mountains were easy? Hard as nails seniors who had something to prove, of course.

The point, as it turned out, was not that these mountain hikes were simple (though some were) but rather this list explored parts of the state that tourists and 4,000-footer climbers never bothered to visit, to say nothing of hiking the trails. And each mountain, somewhere, provided a stunning vista.

Over the course of our travels, Janelle and I put more than 225 miles on our boots, and many more miles than that on our car. We hiked as far north as the Canadian border. We hiked in the western Connecticut Valley. We discovered dirt and gravel access roads that tested my car's suspension. We hiked on private land, through backyards (always with permission) and down paved paths.

We hiked with purpose; to attain the goal of completing this list, yes. But we found that this quest was really just a means of spending time with each other. Simply saying we bonded is too flip. Spending 24 hours a day with a child, sometimes for four or five days straight, alone, working on a specific project, creates something more than a bond.

We began to understand each other. We watched out for each

other. There was pain and tears and days that seemed designed to work against us. She sacrificed time with her friends, and holidays from school. She did her homework on the rug in our cabin in Whitefield, between unpacking from one hike and getting ready for another.

I also sacrificed time at home, distanced myself from family and friends at times in order to find something deeper and more tangible than checking off a mere list.

And we did, I think. I hope.

WHEN THOSE POLICE ARRIVED, way back in the early days of our hiking, I understood what it felt like to have the full weight of the responsibility of this girl's health and well-being and safety on my shoulders. And how terribly, at that moment, I could have failed her.

As soon as I saw the officer walking up the trail toward us, I knew someone had called something in about us. Before he got within earshot, I pointed out to Janelle that a police officer was on the trail, and spun it as a good thing that a back trail like this was being watched over by the police.

And sure enough, according to the officer someone had called the police to report "an older man with a young girl in the woods." Just reading that out loud sounds terrible, but consider that this description could describe any father and daughter taking a hike.

But I'm not Janelle's dad, so when the very polite officer asked me what my relation to Janelle was, I did what I've been taught to do in a situation like this: I told the truth. I said I was a next-door neighbor, but then I made the mistake of saying I was doing the "big brother thing" for Janelle. The officer took that to mean the Big Brother/Big Sister Program. By now a second officer had shown up, and when Janelle's grandma was called for verification, the police dispatcher did not give her grandmother my name, but instead asked if Janelle was currently with someone from the city's Big Brother/Big Sister Program. Grandma said no, Janelle was with Meena Gyawali.

My heart sank. This was slipping away fast. As a third officer arrived, images of me being hauled off in handcuffs and Janelle freaking out were all that I could think of.

I tried to remain casual and conversational. I explained that Meena was my wife, and grandma likely just didn't realize that we had each taken one of the kids out this morning. I politely suggested that the dispatcher give grandma my name. That did the trick. The officer asked Janelle a few direct questions: was she happy, did she hike a lot with me, was she OK being out here, etc. After twenty tense minutes, they let us go.

In retrospect, after a year plus of hiking, with a guardian permission slip from Janelle's grandmother always in my pocket, the incident seems ridiculous.

But it wasn't and it still shakes me when I think about how fine the line is that we always walk when we live in a world where an older man with a young girl out for a hike is indeed a questionable thing.

On one hand, someone cared enough to see us together, feel concern for the child and call the police.

On the other hand, it's a reminder that we live in a time where everything is questioned. Had I actually been her father, would that have made the situation easier to deal with? What does that say about the role of an adult supervisor? Should I pick only "safe" activities for the child where no one would question our being together?

In the time that we've been together hiking, no one has ever questioned it again. Most often, in fact, the assumption is that I'm Janelle's dad, a situation that neither of us bothers to correct as the explanation of what we actually are is long and complicated.

As for Janelle, she's a tough kid who has the ability to put incidents like the police questioning into perspective. In fact, an early potential trail name for her was *cop magnet*. (Ultimately, her trail name was given to her by her brother, who after an argument about her hiking speed told her, "You think you're such a tough cookie!")

Both Janelle and I now see that incident with the police as a crossroads. A little bit in one direction, and I would have been carted off and Janelle and I would never have hiked again. But it didn't go that way. Instead, it bought us closer together as we considered the fact that sometimes, being a family goes deeper than blood—sometimes being a family just means caring for each other.

WE HOPE in the pages ahead that you find your own peace and joy in the simple act of walking. Some of these mountains are very easy, the trails designed and trodden upon so deeply and often that anyone can climb to the lookouts. In some cases, the climb is as difficult as or more so than any 4,000-footer and should not be done without preparation and great caution.

I wrote *The Adventures of Buffalo and Tough Cookie* not as a definitive guide to this list, but rather as a story between two friends. But the narrative of the mountains can be anyone's.

New Hampshire is a beautiful place. Janelle and I are very fortunate to live so near to such challenging beauty. Also, we've been able to take advantage of the endless support given to us by our mutual families, who early on recognized this deeply personal project as something we both needed, the lasting effects of which I hope will echo throughout the rest of Janelle's life.

But no matter where you are, no matter what you do, the lessons are universal. Learn the terrain. Find comfort in the everyday. Discover. And persevere.

*The Adventures of Buffalo
and Tough Cookie*

| 1 |

First Steps

On our first hike of the 52 With a View list, I make a tactical error that nearly ends our entire journey. Kearsarge Mountain Road is closed for the winter, and we are forced to begin our hike with a road walk.

Normally, even in off season (or so I thought), this road that leads to Winslow State Park is open for most of its length, up to the state park toll gate. But today, despite the clear-of-snow road, there is a locked chain blocking my car.

"What do we do?" Janelle asks.

Go home, I want to say. "We hoof it," I do say.

So, on a cold but cloudless November day, Janelle and I take our first steps toward Mt. Kearsarge and toward a journey that will ultimately change both our lives, though we don't know this yet.

I walk up the road with this child, pointing out late-season chipmunks, trying to gauge how easily, or not, she gets cold. I have no clue how this is done. I have no clue who Janelle is. She *is* eager, and strong. That much I know from the few small hikes we've taken prior to this big one. And she does not complain easily.

I've never hiked a serious mountain with a child before. Alone. So, I've loaded my backpack with so much emergency gear, it feels like we could be out in the woods for weeks.

The road is only a mile to the trailhead, but she begins asking me when we'll get there about half way up. I wonder if this is going to work. "Is this the trail?" she wants to know. "Are we hiking?" Though short, the road slog feels interminable, but once we crest the small rise and enter the actual park with its playground equipment and picnic benches, Janelle perks up.

Winslow State Park is named after the nineteenth century hotel that used to sit right on the park's current picnic area. The hotel was named after Admiral John Winslow, who commanded the USS *Kearsarge* during the Civil War and became famous for sinking the Confederate raider the CSS *Alabama*. Tying all this history up into a fine knot is the odd tidbit that when Admiral Winslow died in Boston, a slab of stone from Mt. Kearsarge was sent down to cover his grave.

The good admiral remains in our thoughts as we finally tackle the Winslow Trail and begin our climb, a 1.1-mile hike to the bare ledges and Kearsarge's fire tower. We move under some power lines and the trail becomes steep, switching between rock stair climbing and moving over icy, damp rock slabs.

We chat a bit and I let her lead, but she's hesitant despite the well-trodden path.

"Is everything okay?" I ask.

She's looking up the trail, side to side. "I, um, I'm not sure where to go."

And then it hits me. There is no difference to her between trail and forest. She's a child of the city, of the concrete alley. To me, the Winslow Trail is as clear as if it were a paved superhighway. To Janelle, this is new: the trees, the rocks, the ice. She has no context for her brain to understand "trails" vs. "woods."

So our first lesson begins. I sit beside her and we talk about blazes and cairns. I find several of the red blazes and we go right up to the tree or rock and I have her touch the blaze. And as we begin to move again, she picks up speed, emboldened by the knowledge of direction. She moves to the next blaze, and the next. We take a small break every 10 or 15 blazes, and it becomes a game.

And suddenly, I understand as well. To begin this journey with her, a hike must be small and personal, a space of 30 or 50 feet at a time.

Tough Cookie rests up after her first hike up a 52er, Mount Kearsarge.

A hike is figuring out what's around the next corner only, and going there. After fifteen years of hiking, in the first mile of a walk with this nine-year-old, I learn the most important lesson of all. Slow down.

We hike like this, counting blazes, as the trail swings up Kearsarge's northeastern slope and past our first lookout called Halfway Rock. The mud becomes icy, but the sun beats down and it never really gets too cold. Before long we pop out on the open ledges.

Then, as the radio tower rises before us, then the fire tower, then the vast 360-degree views, Janelle slows her pace. I give her a minute and allow her to take in this magnificent mountain on her terms. I wish I were inside her head. I wish I could stand atop a mountain again for the first time. I hope she feels the same as I did.

She slowly turns, and it seems like all of New England spreads out before us. When she finally turns toward me, I hold my breath. She smiles and holds up her hand, palm out.

It's the most satisfying high-five I've ever experienced.

Mt. Kearsarge   *Nov. 5, 2011*

SUMMIT ELEVATION 2,930 feet

LOCATION AND DIRECTIONS Wilmot. From I-89, take to Exit 10, then proceed
north on Kearsarge Valley Road to Kearsarge Mountain Road and the
entrance sign to Winslow State Park. Turn right here and continue to
trailhead near the site of the old Winslow House.

OUR ROUTE The Winslow Trail (also sometimes called the Northside Trail),
up and back. (Warning: Assume Kearsarge Mountain Road will be
closed sometime by mid-October, in which case add a two-mile round
trip road walk to your journey.)

TRIP MILEAGE 4.2 miles round trip, including the road walk.

IF YOU GO Mt. Kearsarge can be reached from two sides, Winslow State
Park in Wilmot and Rollins State Park in Warner. From the Winslow
side, the 1.7-mile Barlow Trail also reaches the summit. From the Rollins
State Park side, an auto road (closed in winter) rises from the park
entrance and ends a half mile from the summit. From there, take the
Rollins Trail.

There are entrance fees during summer hours at both parks. Check
www.nhstateparks.org for more information.

| 2 |

Settle Into the Rock

#2: Welch and Dickey Mountains

I need to get better at this whole gear thing.

We are hiking in late November, and it looks like actual winter will never get here. The Welch-Dickey Trail loop is snowless, but the mud is hard. We move slowly, as Janelle's brother, Aaron, is with us. But knowing that I'd have both kids, and that White Mountain weather is notorious for turning on a dime, I've brought my weekend pack.

I am like a thru hiker, a Grand Canyon explorer; I may as well be carrying both those kids on my back. The normally easy-going, 4.4-mile Welch-Dickey Trail Loop pulls at my legs, and within 100 yards I'm bathed in sweat.

I must have put all my gear in there.

Our friends Neil and Steve began this hike with us but left to find their own fortunes, our pace far too slow for their liking.

I'm startled at how many mushrooms and other fungi exist on a trail. Janelle and Aaron find all of it, every last stem and sprout. And colored leaves. And bugs. And look at that weirdly shaped tree. And what creature lives in this hole?

The boy is able to identify more flora than I am. I can't answer their questions about simple tree identification. I'm in trouble here.

I've hiked to Everest Base Camp. I've climbed all 48 of New Hampshire's 4,000-footers in 20 days. But this is different. This is micro-hiking.

Heading down the ledges of Welch and Dickey Mountains, Tough Cookie is still using her pink polka-dotted school backpack.

I consider simply letting them run into the woods ten feet from the trailhead and sitting down on a rock and waiting until they are done. It would be the most deeply explored 100 square feet of forest in all the White Mountains. After three hours, they would be able to write their college thesis on that patch of land.

This would make Aaron very happy. The boy has ocular albinism, a genetic condition that reduces the pigmentation of the iris. One result is difficulty with depth perception, which makes hiking on New Hampshire's notoriously rooty and rocky trails a trial.

But he tries, oh, how the boy tries. After a little more than a mile, the trail opens to the first set of wide ledges with fine views toward the Tripyramids, and we take a break to drink some hot chocolate and figure out how to proceed. Meenakshi is with us, and Aaron has had enough. They decide to return to the car.

But Janelle is different. She stands there looking up at the summit crown of Welch, about half a mile away. I know that look, can feel that same pull. That longing look is the first signal to me that this may be something big I have on my hands.

"Can we keep going?" she asks.

The weather is a little shakier than two weeks ago atop Kearsarge, and I'm reluctant to split up our group. But Meena says go, and so we part. We hug all around, an important moment, significant to Janelle's and my journey. We turn our backs on our partners, lift our heads into the wind, and make for the lower of the two summits.

The slabs on Welch are wet, and in some cases icy, but Janelle brings her body close to the rock and climbs like instinct is her guide. I teach her to find footholds, to test roots for give. I force her to stop and turn around every so often, to look out over the Sandwich Range and absorb this day.

The wind picks up but we have gear and the weather never turns. That half mile up Welch is some of the finest low-level hiking anywhere in New Hampshire, full of slides, ledges, rock squeezes and harrowing cliffs.

Before long, we scramble to the top of the Welch summit and the November wind whistles over that little summit area, but the girl steps up onto that rock, a little thing in an oversized pink winter coat and princess stocking hat, and she suddenly seems much larger to me.

She grins and breaks out some cinnamon doughnut bites for a snack.

"Are we going over there?" she asks, pointing across the col to Dickey, the true summit of this mountain.

"Yup," I say, "then down those rocky ledges over there, then back around to Aaron and Meena."

"Great," she says. "Want a doughnut?"

Welch & Dickey Mtns.   *Nov. 20, 2011*

SUMMIT ELEVATION Welch, 2,605 ft.; Dickey, 2,734 ft.

LOCATION AND DIRECTIONS Near Waterville Valley. Take I-93 to Exit 28. Follow Route 49 (toward Waterville Valley) approximately 4.5 miles, then turn left (west) onto Upper Mad River Road. In 0.7 mi. turn right onto Orris Road and proceed another 0.6 mi. to the trailhead parking lot.

OUR ROUTE The Welch-Dickey Loop Trail, up and back.

TRIP MILEAGE 4.4 miles round trip.

IF YOU GO The Welch-Dickey loop is a fine hike over two excellent peaks with a single trail that crosses both summits and loops back down. You can go in either direction, though the common route is counterclockwise so as to make Dickey, the higher of the two summits, your final peak. Be prepared for a crowd at any time of year. The loop hike over Welch and Dickey is one of the most common starter or tourist hikes in New Hampshire, for good reason. The views are outstanding for the effort. Beware, though; in winter, these "little" summits, with their long exposed ledges requiring much rock scrambling, can be every bit the challenge of their bigger cousins.

| 3 |

The Birth of a Peakbagger

#3: Mount Monadnock

Four months have passed since Janelle and I have touched a mountain. She's begged me to hike nearly every week since our last excursion in November, and I've understood her desire. But a hernia and subsequent operation and recovery have grounded me.

Now, on one of the warmest March days on record, the pull of the mountains is too great to resist. We have a prior commitment later this afternoon, which means we don't have time for a lot of travel. The closest mountain to us is the great Monadnock. I worry that it may be a little early in Janelle's experience to tackle a 3,000-footer, but the perfect blue-bird day is too glorious to miss.

Still, we have to wake up at 4:30 AM to have enough time to climb this lovely and popular mountain. You'd think that waking up a nine-year-old at that hour would be a Herculean effort, but so excited is Janelle to do this climb that she sleeps in most of her hiking clothes and gulps down her morning Cheerios standing up so she can get on the road faster.

It is the earliest she has ever woken up (which to a kid is really like staying up late).

Another bonus of such an early day: We have Monadnock nearly to ourselves all the way up, through morning mist, low-lying clouds and even a sunrise. As those familiar with Monadnock know, climbing this mountain can sometimes feel like being in a city bus station — droves of hikers of pretty much every level of readiness (including none) attempt to haul themselves up Monadnock. Indeed, on the way down, we will come across all level of hikers.

But the way up is glorious. High spirits. Beautiful warm day. A variety of terrain — rock, mud, ice, snow. The girl is in her element with so much rock, bombing over the ledges, practically bursting with energy at the rock-scrambling opportunities.

As I huff and puff to keep up with her, my legs heavy from inactivity, it occurs to me that I'm behind the curve here. My surgery took more out of me than I had thought. I will only be able to keep pace with her for a while longer if she continues like this.

She surprises me in two ways on this climb. First, as we sit, nearly alone at the summit after a casual three-hour hike up, she mentions that sitting on a summit sipping raspberry tea has become her favorite part of our hikes. It pleases me to know she's developing her own rituals — to me, crucial way-marks on any hike.

Second, I believe I am witnessing the birth of a peakbagger. Monadnock is our first hike up a mountain that involves more than one trail. We took the White Dot to the White Cross. On previous hikes, one trail led to each of the summits.

Here, Janelle spends a lot of time asking me odd questions like "Where does the mountain start?" and "Why is there more than one trail?" before I realize that in her experience thus far *every* trail has led to a summit.

"Can't we just take the trail that goes to the top?" she asks. A learning moment, and the birth, I think, of the peakbagger in my new climbing partner.

The way down is more eventful, with a series of brush burns and bruises to accompany what by then is one tired little hiker. A round trip to Monadnock is only 4.4 miles, but Janelle has no concept of pace or timing. But we stop to rest and eat often, and celebrate those bings and bumps like the badges of honor they are. She lets me take all the weight out of her pack, and before long she is literally skipping back to the car.

Every hike for now is a learning experience of one sort or another,

We break the 3,000-foot mark atop Mount Monadnock.

and my goal at this stage is to get her up a 4,000-footer. But as we head home, and Janelle immediately falls asleep in the car, neither of us knows that very soon her growing interest in hiking will turn our occasional adventure into a full-blown mountain pilgrimage.

Mt. Monadnock   *March 18, 2012*

SUMMIT ELEVATION 2,734 feet

LOCATION AND DIRECTIONS Jaffrey. From Jaffrey's village center, follow Route 124 West 2.3 mi. to Dublin Road. Turn right here and drive 1.3 mi. to Poole Road and the entrance to Monadnock State Park. The trailhead parking lot is reached in another 0.7 mi.

OUR ROUTE The White Dot to White Cross trails, up and back.

TRIP MILEAGE 4.4 miles round trip.

IF YOU GO Monadnock is what it is. Legend has it this popular peak near Jaffrey is the second-most-climbed mountain in the world, second only to Mt. Fuji in Japan. You'll have more luck finding solitude in a public pool than on Mt. Monadnock in the summer. However, the mountain is popular for a reason.

It's challenging, there's a variety of terrain, and if you don't mind sharing your day with others, nothing can beat this state park. And, with more than 40 miles of trails, you can find some solitude on trails like Lost Farm or Marlboro.

Janelle and I took one of the most popular routes, the White Dot to the White Cross, 4.4 miles total. But the variety of trail options is tremendous and appropriate for any level of fitness. Want a challenge? Try the Pumpelly Trail from Dublin Lake. Good rock scrambles? The Spellman Trail off Cascade Link fits that bill. Don't let the mountain's popularity fool you, though. The exposure and rock scrambles can make this climb as easy or as difficult as your comfort level.

It's a state park, so there is a fee, but given the wonderful condition of the park and the trails (not to mention a visitors' center and exhibits) it still seems like a deal. Upon entering (if you get there during business hours) you'll get a trail map. Please check the website, though, before you go, for winter vs. summer hours and events: www.nhstateparks.org

| 4 |

The Rare Beauty of a Perfect Hike

#4: Black Mountain (Benton)

Isn't it wonderful when nothing goes wrong? When there's no drama? When you're on time, the weather cooperates and a hike gives you everything you hope for?

That is the case for peak No. 4, as Janelle and I drive out to Benton to hike Black Mountain. I asked her to do the research and give me a short list of potential hikes for the day, and Black ended up being the one closest to our Whitefield cabin and a short enough trail to beat the rain that is expected for later in the afternoon. It is the first time we will be tackling a mountain neither one of us has climbed before.

Given the relative ease of the trail and the fact that every single thing we planned fell into place, there isn't much drama to the hike, but we both agree that there's absolutely nothing wrong with a perfect hike.

We are up and out the door by 6 AM and a chilly trailhead temperature of 25 degrees has us bundled up pretty good at the start, but once the sun fully comes up, the layers come off.

The Chippewa Trail is a wonderful, well-worn, wide and well-marked trail that skirts the border of Benton State Forest. The lower half mile is a fascinating maze of marshland, beaver dams and gnarly root structures towering over our heads in some places. Bright orange and yellow fungus and spores glitter like gold dripping off bark in the

Feeling joy near the summit of Black Mountain in Benton.

morning sun, and we explore an old cellar hole about 0.6 miles into the trail.

After the cellar hole, the trail takes a sharp left and begins to climb at easy to moderate grades throughout. In fact, at one point we feel like we're hiking our beloved local mountains, the Uncanoonucs in Goffstown — steep, but on mostly pine needle-covered solid earth.

After about 1.5 miles, we come upon the first of many, many view points on this fine trail and take a break to soak in the remaining sun and hydrate up for the remaining push to the summit.

At that point, a series of ledges and false summits takes us up, up, up and the views appear seemingly around every corner, including one that looks up to the summit rocks.

Soon, we break out onto the glorious summit ledge, which extends a good 100 feet in every direction and faces the unique western side of Mt. Moosilauke. We explore a little, trying to find all the remaining metal pegs of the old fire tower that used to grace the summit, then settle back for a well-earned picnic of raspberry tea, apples, cheese sticks and PB&Js.

We're thrilled when The Feathered Hat, a fellow hiker from one of the online hiking forums, and his two large pups come up to join us.

They are the only mammals we'll see on the trail until nearly the end of our day.

Polly the dog immediately joins our picnic and gives Janelle's well-crafted and delicious sandwiches her stamp of approval by pulling one right out of the baggie and gobbling it up in two bites.

Janelle's shocked expression quickly morphs to laughter and later, when anyone asks how the hike went, the sandwich-stealing pup takes center stage, views be darned!

Feathered Hat feels bad, but we have plenty of snacks and are happy to share with hungry Polly.

The way down is equally mellow and we happily make up songs about killer grouse to pass the time. Janelle continues to get stronger at a scary pace. In contrast to our trip up Monadnock, today she refuses to let me carry any of her weight despite some shoulder pain and achy feet. She makes it clear she wishes to finish on her own, and she does.

It may be time to begin the search for gear that fits her.

Black Mountain (Benton) *April 1, 2012*

SUMMIT ELEVATION 2,830 feet

LOCATION AND DIRECTIONS Haverhill and Benton. From Route 116 near Center Haverhill, turn east onto Lime Kiln Road and drive 1.8 mi. to the parking area and trailhead. Alternately, the Chippewa Trail can be reached from Route 25 in East Haverhill. Turn north onto Lime Kiln Road 5.2 mi. from Glencliff village and drive 3.1 mi. to the trailhead, which is on your right just after a sharp left turn in the road.

OUR ROUTE The Chippewa Tail, up and back. (Warning: Lime Kiln Road could be difficult in wet or winter weather.)

TRIP MILEAGE 3.4 miles round trip.

IF YOU GO There are two options for getting to the summit of Black Mountain, one being the Chippewa Trail and the other the Black Mountain Trail from Howe Hill Road in Benton. The Chippewa Trail, however, is considered the more scenic of the two. At only 1.8 miles one way, it never really climbs steeply, but offers a variety of lookouts and interesting trail diversions along the way. Plus, it offers some classic

New England ledges and a spectacular view of neighboring Mount Moosilauke. Black Mountain may top out at less than 3,000 feet, but its bare summit ledges make it seem like you're much higher.

Be careful during spring, when the hard mud on Lime Kiln Road often turns muddy with sloppy ruts. There is a small parking area at the trailhead that fits about three cars.

| 5 |

Facing the Heat

> #5: Middle Sugarloaf

Sometimes, it's just too hot to do anything but jump in a lake.

But despite the stifling heat, I'm able to use the following line on this hike: "Here's a trick I learned in the Grand Canyon."

After a late evening of Thai food the day before and a too-long sleep-in that morning, Janelle and I decide to continue our quest with a short hike up Middle Sugarloaf, a 2,539-foot mountain just ten miles from the cabin.

Two close friends, Peter and Elizabeth, whose trail names are Alvin the Swede and Inchworm, decide to brave the heat and come along for the fun.

For May, the heat is startling. When we set foot on the Sugarloaf Trail off Zealand Road at 10 AM, the temps are already in the high 60s. By the afternoon, the mercury would rise to nearly 90!

This kind of mountain heat has a way of sucking the life out of you. So, as Janelle and I continue our mutual hiking education, Sunday's hike comes down to hydration. The kid's getting stronger with each hike, but on this hike she learns the valuable lesson of pacing. Heat can slow you down and hurt you as much as snow or rain.

The trail to Middle Sugarloaf is less than 1.5 miles, pleasant, and view-filled; it offers one of the finest views for the effort in the Whites. Janelle takes to the trail like a hiking machine, pounding up the track with a purpose. I mention to Peter that pretty soon the only thing

Janelle makes quick work of the wooden staircase near the summit of Middle Sugarloaf.

she'll need from me is a ride to and from the trailhead. But the heat slows her, and us, down and it doesn't take long for her to understand that on the trail we truly are beholden to the weather. That's when I'm able to use my Grand Canyon line. A couple of years ago, on the way out of the Grand Canyon, I had a dreadful allergic reaction to ibuprofen. Meena soaked a bandana for me and wrapped it around my neck. The cooling cloth made a huge difference. Today I do the same for Janelle. Once she gets over the initial impact of the water and it's dripping down her neck, it seems to give her an extra boost to get comfortably to the ridge.

Once attaining the ridge, the trail splits. To the right (north), the hike to the top of North Sugarloaf is only a 0.6-mile round trip, but no one wants to fight the heat any more than necessary. So we skip North Sugarloaf and go left for Middle, the higher summit of this double-peaked ridgeline.

Right before the summit, there is a small ladder up a steep ledge, the first time Janelle has seen such a thing. "The trail is a ladder?" she asks. I'm not sure whether she approves or not.

As usual, the views from Middle Sugarloaf do not disappoint. We lounge for thirty minutes or so, eat lunch and further warm ourselves on the hot rocks. The breeze from the top barely makes a dent, and it doesn't take long for Janelle to ask if we have time to take a dip in our pond back at the cabin before we head home. So down we go.

The big lesson of the day: You *bribe* a kid to do something she does not want to do. You give her *incentive* to do something she does want to do! The incentive of spending a half hour in the pond is enough to send Janelle roaring down the trail like a freight train. There are, of course, the mandatory conversations about sticking together as a team and that hydration is important on the way down as well.

But before long, we are down and heading back to Whitefield to cool off.

Middle Sugarloaf   *May 20, 2012*

SUMMIT ELEVATION 2,539 feet

LOCATION AND DIRECTIONS Twin Mountain. From the traffic light in Twin Mountain (at the jct. of Routes 3 and 302), go east on Route 302 and drive 2.3 mi. to Zealand Campground and Zealand Road (Forest Road 16). The trailhead is about a mile up on the right. Parking is in a small lot just before the bridge over Zealand River.

OUR ROUTE Sugarloaf Trail, up and back. (We skipped the side trip to North Sugarloaf.)

TRIP MILEAGE 2.8 miles round trip, Middle Sugarloaf summit only.

IF YOU GO Zealand Road off Route 302 is where you'll find the trailhead. If you go in early spring, this Forest Service–maintained road is likely to be a mess, full of frost heaves and potholes, so take your time. If you go in the winter, Zealand Road is closed. You can park along Route 302 in a big lot several hundred yards east of the campground, then hike up Zealand Road to the trailhead. That will add nearly 2.5 miles extra miles to your round trip hike. The Sugarloaf Loop leaves the west side of the road just beyond the bridge, and it's only 1.4 miles to the summit. An extra 0.3 mi one way will get you to the equally pretty, but lower North Sugarloaf ledges.

Zealand Road is a magnet for family camping. At any time during the summer, campers and tents will be lining the road at the three separate Forest Service campgrounds situated in the immediate area.

| 6 |

A Fateful Decision

> #6: Stinson Mountain

"Neat," Janelle says. Then quickly adds, "but gross."

We are watching a enormous leopard slug ooze its way down the side of a rotting maple. The sight is particularly fascinating as the tree has apparently died from a lightning strike, the split branch still charred black and flaky.

She's repulsed by the four-inch slimy creature but doesn't want to leave. We're nearly a mile up the Stinson Mountain Trail. The day is warm but breezy. We're both feeling strong. We have nowhere to be and plenty of time to get there. So I shrug off my daypack, get out a snack, and together the girl and I settle back to watch a slug crawl across a tree.

And I think to myself, yeah, this really is the life.

We decided to tackle 2,900-foot Stinson without much fanfare yesterday. The trail to the summit is only 1.8 miles, and the grade is moderate all the way. With only about 1,400 feet of elevation gain, we figured Stinson would be a good way for us to set off on a new chapter in our adventure, because we made another decision yesterday as well: We will finish the 52 With a View in one year's time.

Since our first summit, Mount Kearsarge, took place on November 5, 2011, that gives us three and a half months to complete the list. We made this decision with very little thought or consideration behind the toll it would take on us or on our families, or the logistics and planning such a quest would entail.

It just seemed . . . natural.

Early November meant a tight window considering the kid would be back in school for half that time, but we figure we have a solid month of summer to play with, and the two of us are always up for a ridiculous challenge. What we didn't understand then was the impact these next three months would have on our lives, and how different we'd come out on the other side.

So, earlier today as Janelle posed for a shot at the trailhead and flashed that big grin of hers, I said, "Well, it's the beginning of a great adventure, isn't it?"

"Yup," she said, turned her back to me and hit the trail at nearly a run.

The first mile of the Stinson Mountain Trail is a joy, a mainly flat fern glade followed by a moderate climb past some old farm walls onto the shoulder of the mountain. We chatted a little about the old stone walls that wound around and near us, but Janelle seemed less interested in man-made objects found in the forest than the forest itself.

The slug, then, is a pleasant intermission, though neither of us is particularly tired at this point. But I'm trying to teach the kid how to pace her hikes, something she'll need to learn quickly as we proceed down (or up) the list to mountains that will require 8-, 10- or 12-mile hikes. Some of the mountains that remain are climbs as difficult as, if not more so, than their higher, but easier, 4,000-foot sisters.

But for today, there's no stopping her. We power up the remaining 0.9 mile, counting toads as we go (three) and hit the loop junction just below the summit about ninety minutes after we left the trailhead. A sign there for snowmobiles says Go Right, so we do and in five minutes Janelle is clambering up a small ledge — and just like that we're on the summit.

"What's that?" she says.

In 1911, the New Hampshire Timberland Owners built a 16-foot wooden fire tower atop Stinson. That tower was replaced with 27-foot

Summit thumbs up atop an old fire tower foundation on Stinson Mountain.

steel tower with a cab in 1927. The tower was removed in 1985, but the concrete footings remain. But what fascinates Janelle is the concrete steps to nowhere. The steps to the stairs remain at the summit, an odd relic of another time.

And in our case, a perfect table for lunch. So there we sit, and spread our lunch of PB&J, trail mix and blueberries out on the stairs that decades of feet used to climb that tower.

I had read about a view off the west side of the summit to Stinson Lake, so after a while we poke around the summit looking for any hint of a beaten path. It's not hard to find. The herd path leads about thirty feet slightly down slope to a well-trodden clearing where we are able to catch a great view of the lake.

The day is fine, the breeze is perfect to keep bugs away, and neither of us wishes to leave yet, so we climb back to our stairs perch and relax in the sun.

After a time, our reverie is broken by the sound of a family of four kids about Janelle's age reaching the summit. They shout and shove and seem to be having the time of their lives. Soon, a little dog arrives, followed by the hiker we assume is their mom.

Janelle whispers in my ear, "Those kids are loud."

I think about the hike to Bald Peak we took last year with Janelle and Aaron, along with their friends Ian and Meg, and chuckle. Still, I'm glad she's able to recognize how pleasant solitude can be in the mountains.

"Let's get out of here," I say, "and find ourselves some peace and quiet." And so we do.

Stinson Mountain *July 18, 2012*

SUMMIT ELEVATION 2,900 feet

LOCATION AND DIRECTIONS Rumney. From Exit 26 on I-93, take Route 25 West to Rumney and Stinson Lake Road. Once on Stinson Lake Road, drive 5.0 mi. and turn right uphill on Cross Road for 0.8 mi., then go right onto Lower Doe Town Road and continue 0.3 mi. to the trailhead parking lot.

OUR ROUTE Stinson Mountain Trail, up and back.

TRIP MILEAGE 3.6 miles round trip.

IF YOU GO Stinson Mountain Trail is a moderate hike, doable for kids and beginners. Be sure to stick to the trail as there are some snowmobile cut-offs that are not shown on the Appalachian Mountain Club's trail map for this area. The loop at the summit is only a matter of a couple hundred feet around. The trail is accessible year-round.

| 7 |

Ties That Bind

#7: Mount Israel

Janelle and I climb the steep old cart path at the beginning of the Wentworth Trail. The day is hot and the trail is dry.

Wentworth is moderate, a straightforward path with a few switchbacks and not much climbing. A stellar lookout at the 1.5-mile mark gives us a chance to catch our breath. Soon after, ledges begin, including a false summit that seems to baffle Janelle.

"Why is it false?" she asks.

"The mountain has a real, higher summit, over there." I point to the slight rise about a tenth of a mile away.

"Weird."

That true summit does not disappoint, with a variety of ledges to explore and nice pointed mountaintop rock. Janelle settles in near the summit and slips off her boots. Finding her boots that fit has been a challenge, and her feet are beginning to suffer for it.

I occupy myself with lunch as Janelle scampers barefoot to the summit cairn and tosses a handful of trail mix to the wind. She looks small at the summit, nearly the same size as the cairn marking the top. She pauses for a moment, head down, then scampers back to her lunch. Catching my eye, she shrugs.

"It's for grandpa."

I shake my head, not understanding.

Mount Israel's false summit is still a beautiful ridge walk.

"When I make an offering to the mountain gods, I ask them to keep grandpa safe."

I open my mouth, but nothing comes out.

"What?" she asks. "I do that on every mountain. I think he'd be proud of me for doing this."

There's no piety or religious fervor in her voice or in this action. That offering in his memory is just a thing she does, a way of keeping her grandfather alive in her thoughts, of taking him with her to these places.

I squeeze her shoulder. "He would be," is all I manage to say.

Janelle combines her own offering with one Meena and I practice in the mountains, a sense of reverence for the hills we climb. Religious, or even grounded in reality? No. But perhaps spending a few moments at the top of a mountain considering your place in creation is enough to bring you closer to whatever god you desire. If nothing else, offering M&Ms to the wind at the tops of mountains can be a small moment of wonder, a silent acknowledgment that maybe we don't have all the answers.

Over a year ago, Janelle's grandfather passed away suddenly; it was about that time that she and her brother came into Meena's and my life. She rarely speaks about him in terms of loss. Rather, her grandfather is a constant presence on our hikes and in her life.

Learning about Jim through the memory and eyes of a child has been interesting. He was funny, of course. A practical joker. Afraid of heights.

She doesn't dwell on her moment of captured reverence. There's no need. The mountain is under us, we are together surrounded by the rolling hills of the Sandwich Wilderness and all is calm and well.

There is no loss here.

Later as we begin the hike down, we come across three hikers on the false summit, two women and a girl younger than Janelle. They are confused.

"Is this the summit?" one asks me.

I explain that the true summit is only a tenth of a mile away and has better ledge views. But they are in a hurry, and despite the pleas from the little girl, they are not going forward, not touching a summit so close.

We leave them, and Janelle is quiet for a while.

"Why didn't her mom want to go to the summit?" she asks. "They were so close."

"Maybe they had other commitments or they ran out of time."

This is not acceptable to her. "But, if we were that close, we'd go to the summit, right?"

I pause, sensing the minefield ahead. "If the weather was good like this, and we had time like we do today, then, yeah, of course, we'd always go to the summit."

She turns to look at me, as if to judge my sincerity, my summit chops. "Good," she says, and turns back to the trail.

Mt. Israel

July 22, 2012

SUMMIT ELEVATION 2,630 feet

LOCATION AND DIRECTIONS Near Center Sandwich. From Center Sandwich, follow Sandwich Mountain Road 2.5 mi. before turning right onto Diamond Ledge Road, which leads in 0.4 mi. to Mead Conservation Center, a trail crew camp used by the Wonalancet Outdoor Club and Squam Lakes Association and operated by the Friends of Mead. Park your vehicle in a field in front of the camp.

OUR ROUTE Wentworth Trail, up and back.

TOTAL MILEAGE 4.2 miles round trip.

IF YOU GO The Wentworth Trail is not easy to find, but folks in Sandwich like it that way. We took a wrong turn on a maze of hard-pack dirt roads and had to ask a kind couple out for a walk where the Mead Conservation Center was located.

| 8 |

Indian Head of the Notch

#8: Mount Pemigewasset

Since the Old Man fell from his Cannon Mountain perch in 2003, the visage on Pemigewasset known as Indian Head has begun to play a more prominent role in New Hampshire tourism.

This may have something to do with the good folks at the Indian Head Resort at the foot of the mountain, who eagerly push the name and this natural feature.

But because this mountain's summit cliffs have become known as Indian Head, it's widely thought that the name, Pemigewasset, is the name of a Native American chief. It is not.

"Pemigewasset" is an Abenaki word meaning "rapidly moving," a reference not to a chief but to the Pemigewasset River, which flows out from the Franconia Ridge.

No matter. From a spot near the resort, there's no denying that the cliffs, our summit, look like an Indian head. I slow the car as we pass to show Janelle.

"Oh yeah!" she says.

We had other plans for today, bigger and longer mountains. But the day is wet and muggy and neither of us feels like fighting for a summit today.

The Mount Pemigewasset Trail hooks left off the paved White-house Trail (otherwise known as the Franconia Notch bike trail) and

Tough Cookie prepares to hike under the highway on the way to
Mount Pemigewasset.

crosses under Route 3 and then the lanes of Interstate 93 with three
tunnels — another first for Janelle.

The trail winds up at easy grades, dodging a couple small stream
crossings, growing a bit steeper near the top, then finally breaking out
onto a glorious ledge that overlooks the southern part of Franconia
Notch and I-93.

We are damp and sticky by the time we reach the summit, and curious, swirling, low clouds drip like moss off the surrounding hills.
The dampness hangs in the air, the summit ledges feel slick, our water
warm and salty. It seems like it might rain at any moment, but if it does
it will be a relief.

Janelle slips off her boots and rubs her feet. "My feet hurt."

The last few hikes, and days, I've watched helplessly as her heels
and toes have become red, then raw, then blistery. Buying good hiking boots for a ten-year-old feels like a fool's quest. Clerks at reputable
gear shops have just stared at her and shaken their heads at me, as if to

say, "Why would you be taking this poor, helpless thing to such places to begin with?"

So we've improvised, but not well, apparently. Janelle has used Meena's old boots, a fine pair of women's Asolos. But the kid has big feet, and flat, and they seem to grow visibly every day. And since there are no clown shoes shops, we've done the best we could.

Meanwhile, Janelle kicks around the wide summit area and cliffs. "Don't fall off the mountain, kid," I say, and she looks at me as if I'm mad.

A warm rain comes and goes, and we reluctantly decide it's time to move.

On the way down, we must step off trail for a moment to let a huge group of hikers pass us by, heading up. There are half a dozen kids Janelle's age, a couple little ones and three adults. None of them have water. None of them have a pack. One adult is carrying a two-year-old in his arms.

I keep my mouth shut. The trail is not long, it's still early in the day and there are many hikers around. Having nothing is foolish, but they should be fine today.

Tired, and thirsty, but fine.

One of the adults asks me how far to the top, and I'm honest. I tell them it's still a mile and the real climbing is yet to come.

He seems crestfallen. "The last guy said we were almost there," he sort of whines.

"He lied," I say pleasantly.

The guy laughs uncomfortably at my non-joke and moves on, I suspect wishing that I'm wrong.

"Why'd you say that?" Janelle asks.

"What do you mean?" I ask. "You know how far it is to the top."

"But maybe the other guy didn't know. Or anyway, you could have said it more nicely."

She pouts for a moment, and I'm suddenly thrilled that I found a way to embarrass her! She had a teenage moment, and I was the annoying adult saying the wrong thing. That's a whisper of our future, perhaps, a moment of comfortable tension I understand to suggest a bond, her rolling her eyes at something the old man said. How about that?

"What's so funny?" she says.

"Nothing, kid-o," I say. "I'll be nicer next time, I promise."

I can't stop grinning for the rest of the hike out.

Mt. Pemigewasset *July 29, 2012*

SUMMIT ELEVATION 2,557 feet

LOCATION AND DIRECTIONS Franconia Notch State Park. From I-93 North, take Exit 34A to Route 3 and proceed a short distance north to the Flume Visitor Center. The closest parking to the trailhead is in the northwest corner of the lot.

OUR ROUTE Franconia Notch Recreation Path (bike path) to Mt. Pemigewasset Trail, up and back.

TRIP MILEAGE 3.8 miles round trip.

IF YOU GO Don't be fooled by this mountain's proximity to the Flume Visitor Center or its low mileage. The Mt. Pemigewasset Trail has some fairly steep pitches and sheer drop-offs at the top. If you're up there with little ones, keep an eye on them. The mountain is a great winter hike as well, and easily accessible at all times of the year. An alternate route to the summit is the Indian Head Trail, which begins on the west side of Route 3, 0.2 mi. north of Indian Head Resort. This approach is just a hair shorter distance-wise from our chosen route, but includes 300 additional feet of vertical ascent.

| 9 |

Of Feet, Strangers and Yoga

#9: Mount Hedgehog

"Really," Janelle says, "all we're going to need is some moleskin, tape and a little luck!"

The hike up to Mt. Hedgehog begins with a discussion of her ongoing battle with what I call beginner's hiking feet. Our hikes now begin with me bandaging her feet in the parking lot.

Blisters, corns, cuts, bruises, scratches: you name it. Since we started this journey, she's had them all. At first, they caused her pain. Then they annoyed her. Now, she muscles through them, seasoned and not caring.

In fact, the night before, she casually mentioned that she "banged" her foot playing at the pool. I was horrified to discover a quarter-size lesion, half brush-burn, half bruise, on the front of her ankle.

"Janelle, my gosh!" I said.

She only shrugged and commanded, "Just tape it up, Dan!"

Her tenacity is admirable, and she certainly appears to be living up to her trail name, but there is one black, round blister-like mole on her foot that concerns me. Perhaps the bruise is a corn. We noticed it a week or so ago, and the thing is just getting bigger, and more red and inflamed. I use a blister doughnut patch to tape it, then wrap muscle tape around her whole foot. The makeshift first aid seems to work, but that foot is going to need to be looked at.

Part of the problem, of course, is that her feet are growing. This boot thing is going to be an expensive problem, I fear.

Pausing for a yoga Tree Pose on the ledges of Hedgehog Mountain.

Our path today is the UNH Trail, named for the former University of New Hampshire Forestry Camp that was located nearby. We decide on the counterclockwise loop, which swings us up a gentle slope to a lookout called Allen's Ledge. Janelle bolts straight up the rock, fueled perhaps by memories of the ledge climbing on Monadnock that she loved so much. I follow, and soon we are standing on a rock with no views.

"What the heck?" she says. "You said there would be views."

But before I can puzzle things out, we hear a voice from below us and through some trees. "Down here," he calls. "Better views from down here."

A short scramble later, we are standing on a flat rock with magnificent views so far east we can see the shadowy tip of far off Mount Washington. The voice belongs to a middle-aged man perched at the end of the rock. He's old-school, with well-used hiking clothes and deep sun lines around his eyes.

"That's better," he says. "Not bad, huh?"

We peer into the valley, trying to pick out the Kancamagus Highway and other landmarks.

"Here," he says to Janelle. "Use these." He slips a pair of binoculars off his neck and holds out his hand. She is thrilled but looks at me first, and for one heavy moment I become fully aware of the weight of my responsibility toward this child. This man is friendly, enthusiastic and harmless. And most will be. But he's only the first of many, many strangers we will encounter, and I'll have to pass judgment on each and every one of them.

That's a task I imagine every parent or guardian, everywhere, makes every day, all the time. I swallow hard.

"Go ahead," I say. "Careful, though; don't break them."

The day rolls by as our trail winds us up to Hedgehog's pleasant series of summit ledges. I point out future hikes as we eat our bagels and peanut butter — Chocorua, Square Ledge on Passaconaway, and Potash, tomorrow's hike.

The loop swings us down off the summit and around to the mountain's south-facing cliffs. The breeze and views are nice here, and Janelle suddenly says, "Here, watch this."

She lifts her arms above her head and crooks one leg into a near-perfect Yoga Tree Pose.

"Where did you learn to do that?" I ask, impressed.

She shrugs. "My Wii yoga game."

Perfect. Video game technology atop a mountain. "Do that again," I say.

"There are other poses I can do."

"No, that one is perfect. I like that one."

She moves into her tree pose there on the warm ledges of this fine, small mountain, and I can't help but feel like this might work out after all.

Mt. Hedgehog   *August 7, 2012*

SUMMIT ELEVATION 2,532 feet

LOCATION AND DIRECTIONS Albany. The short trailhead access road is located
    off the scenic Kancamagus Highway — almost directly across from the
    White Mountain National Forest's Passaconaway Campground — and is
    commonly referred to as the Downes Brook Trail parking lot.

OUR ROUTE UNH Trail loop. Be aware that a section of the eastern part of the loop has been relocated, and the sign at the loop junction is a bit confusing.

TOTAL MILEAGE 4.8 miles round trip.

IF YOU GO We made the full loop, but an up-and-back to the summit can be as short as 3.4 miles. The UNH Trail is about as mellow and moderate a hike as any to be found in the Whites. Its proximity to the popular Kanc Highway makes it ideal for families or beginners looking for a fine view with minimal effort.

Girl vs. Plantar Wart

"This might pinch a little," the doctor says to Janelle just before he cuts into her foot.

She looks at her grandmother, then over at me.

It's gonna hurt, I mouth. Her eyes widen. *But you're tough,* I finish.

Of all the indignities a ten-year-old girl has to face in the normal day to day of being a ten-year-old girl, developing a plantar wart on your foot is usually not high on the list.

But over the course of the past month, the tiny, throbbing, blister-like sore on her foot bloomed into a full-on wart; round, thick, red and gross. We tried over-the-counter medication, which seemed to help, but every time we'd shrink the damn thing, it would just grow back, deeper and more painful than before.

On our hikes, I'd use a circular blister pad with a doughnut hole in the middle. I'd put the hole over the wart, then wrap her foot in athletic tape. It mostly worked, but the thing was just getting bigger.

Ironically, of course, it was likely all the hiking that gave her the wart to begin with.

Plantar warts are actually viruses, occurring on the feet, and incubated in wet or moist (or sweaty) shoes. Yeah, being a hiker basically.

So we finally decided that to continue our quest, this disgusting little creature needed to be eradicated. And that meant getting out the knife.

Because these little buggers have roots, like a weed, you gotta go in deep or they'll just come back.

The doctor is a kind, white-haired fellow, who talks Janelle through the topical anesthesia and then seems amused when she asks, "How soon can I hike?"

He looks at me. "She likes to hike," I say.

Grandma says, "Dan's her hiking partner. They climb mountains."

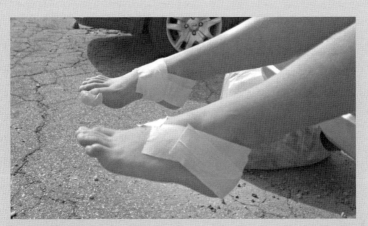

Pre-hike prep work on Janelle's feet at the Webster–Jackson trailhead at Crawford Notch.

He gives the sort of shrug that suggests he doesn't quite understand but is not going to go there. "Oh, she ought to be back on her feet in a couple days."

This causes all of us to breathe a sigh of relief.

It turns out that the cutting part is not too bad. There's a little pain near the end, but she grits her teeth and gets through it. And almost immediately she says she can feel a difference.

For the remainder of our journey, that wart stays dead. We still had blisters, a sprained ankle, a bruised knee and a major lump on the forehead caused by a swing-set seat waiting in our future, but after the cutting, my athletic tape spending binge stops.

She hobbles back to the car, doing calculations in her head. "So, we're hiking this weekend, right?"

"Yup," I say.

She works out the "couple days off your feet" part, nods her head authoritatively as she hops into the car, and lets me close the door behind her.

| 10 |

We Discover Our Spirit

#10: Mount Potash

"Jump," I tell Janelle over the roar of the water. "You can do this."

She's attempting her first bridgeless water crossing. We're halfway across, but she's stalled at a tricky three-foot jump. She makes jumps like this all the time in soccer, running, or just playing in the backyard. But she's never done it with a pack, over the loud rushing current of Downes Brook.

"Go ahead," I say and reach my hand halfway to her over the water. "I'll catch you if you slip."

She takes a deep breath, and leaps. Turns out we're both wrong.

She doesn't have enough forward momentum, and as her foot lands she immediately begins to fall backward, her arms pinwheeling wildly. Without an arm to grab, I take hold of one of the shoulder straps of her pack. But she followed my directions before we began crossing and unhooked the waist strap of her pack, so my hold only throws us both off balance.

And now we're both tipping toward the water. I brace myself against a nearby rock, but not fast enough to prevent her from going in with one foot well past the lip of her trail runner. I'm able to yank her out of the water before we both go in, but her foot and shoe are soaked through.

We climb up onto the shore and evaluate.

"Ugh, I'm soaked!" she moans. "Why isn't there a bridge there?"

Having lunch at the summit near a survey marker on Mount Potash.

I can't help laughing, and it frustrates her even more.

"I'm soaked!"

"I know, kid, but stuff like this happens. We have an extra pair of socks. It's a warm day; your foot will dry in no time," I say. "Still, if you think you can't hike, we can go back."

We're less than a half mile up the Mt. Potash Trail, but I want her to begin thinking for herself. How does she feel? What is she capable of? I want her to start to recognize the difference between problems that can be overcome and problems that force us back.

"No, it's OK," she shakes her foot. "Fine, ugh!"

The day is humid and a thick moisture covers the forest as we work our way up the easy trail. The summit of Potash is wide and filled with warm ledges. We lounge about for a while, but the day is too hot and the mountaintop fails to offer anything worth the sweat.

But on the way down, we come across something that will define the rest of our trip. "Whoa!" Janelle says as she steps over a rotting log. "Look at that."

We discover a leopard slug convention. There are half a dozen of the slimy creatures crawling this way and that. Like we did on Mount Stinson, we take a moment to watch this slow, sticky dance.

"That's it," I say, "this is our spirit animal."

"What's that?"

I explain the shamanic concept of having a power animal that represents a person's connection to all life and empowers them. In shamanic tradition, the spirit animal is essential for the success of any venture. Janelle and I have seen so many of these odd creatures in our journey so far that it seems reasonable, and also, perhaps, a way to connect her more deeply with a respect for the vast variety of life we'll encounter on this trip.

But the idea is over her head. "But it's a slug," she says.

I recalibrate the example in my head. "Uh, think of it like a guardian angel."

"Oh, cool! Spirit animal guardian angel, OK!"

Later, I discover that the slug is actually considered a totem creature, fittingly a harbinger of accomplishing beyond our apparent means because of the slug's surprising ability to climb.

Sure, I'll take whatever we can get.

Mt. Potash   *August 11, 2012*

SUMMIT ELEVATION 2,680 feet

LOCATION AND DIRECTIONS Albany. The short trailhead access road is located along the scenic Kancamagus Highway — almost directly across from the White Mountain National Forest's Passaconaway Campground — and is commonly referred to as the Downes Brook Trail parking lot.

OUR ROUTE Mt. Potash Trail, up and back, via Downes Brook Trail.

TRIP MILEAGE 4.2 miles round trip.

IF YOU GO The Mt. Potash Tail begins at the same trailhead as Hedgehog Mountain and the UNH Trail. Once again, this little mountain offers perfect views and little effort for a reward well worth the meager miles.

| 11 |

Short Does Not Mean Easy

#11: Iron Mountain

As deeply committed and interested as Janelle is in hiking and working on this list, neither of us can escape the irrefutable fact that she's 10 years old.

So sometimes she just can't pull it together. That's fine. If I push too hard, our whole hiking house of cards will collapse. The best-case scenario of that would be we miss our deadline. The worst could be that she never wants to hike again.

For some reason, Potash yesterday exhausted her. Or maybe her head just isn't in it. Or maybe she just wants to go to the candy store in Littleton and spend a buck at the penny counter.

So I scramble to find a short, doable and nearby 52er that we can tick off quickly and have the rest of the day for rest and, perhaps, candy.

Iron Mountain appears to be just what we need.

At less than a mile to the summit, with short side trips available to both lookout ledges and the old mining area that gave the mountain its name, we start up with visions in our heads of how we are going to spend the rest of the day. Boy, do we have a lot to learn.

This little mountain stands tall in history and lore. A ski area once graced the southern side, and a fire tower was used in the thirties and forties. Both are long gone.

And we're surprised to discover that the trail to get to the summit, though short, is exhausting. Deep erosion has carved a thick near-

The trailhead to Iron Mountain offers hikers some of the best views.

tunnel out of the trail, and roots jut out of the soil like hands, pulling us down. Janelle slips on the loose gravel and goes down. She pulls herself up, takes another step, gets tangled in a root structure and goes down again.

"This is terrible," she says.

I move in close behind her, ready to push or grab her as we make our way up the difficult trail. Getting your feet tangled in the open spaces between roots is the quickest way to an injury.

After far too long for such a short trail, we stumble upon the ruins of the old fire tower at the summit. Piles of glass, wood and concrete at the now-wooded summit offer a hint of how grand the views must have been at one time. Now, the tower is a wreck. We pick our way through the refuse, trying to find a spot to sit where there's no glass or rusty nails. We decide instead to continue on, down the south side, where viewpoints await in one direction and the mine ruins can be found in another.

We do find the wide ledges, and the view south toward the Moat Mountain range is lovely. After a quick lunch, we set off to find the ruins of the mine. The trail swoops us steeply down the southeastern flank of the mountain and quickly turns into a poorly marked beaten path.

After twenty minutes of descent on slime-coated rocks, we're running out of patience.

"How are we going to even know what it looks like?" asks Janelle. It's like a moment out of an Indiana Jones movie, because just as she says it we come upon an enormous pit: the old remains of the Iron Mountain mine shaft.

The shaft is thirty feet deep and long, a violent gouge in the side of the slope. Water has pooled at the bottom of the pit, and even in this heat we can feel the cool air rising from the hole, giving off a slight metallic smell.

Suddenly we are aware of the landscape around us. Long-abandoned piles of iron shavings litter the area. I try to imagine this mining operation, but can't. The mountain has taken back most of its form. But the pit is there. We stand at the top for a moment, looking down.

Then Janelle says, "Can we go in?"

We swing down-slope to the front of the pit, the former entrance, I imagine. The walls of the shaft rise up on either side as Janelle and I work our way through weeds and brush and into the man-made ravine. The temperature drops and the shaft walls block out the light. For a few precious steps, we move back in time to when this mountainside was bare and scarred with machinery.

We come to the end of the shaft where water dripping down off the walls has gathered into a deep, black pool. Janelle throws a rock into the pool and we watch the ripples and smell the iron, the two of us there at the bottom of a pit on the side of a mountain.

"Creepy," she says.

"Yup."

"Can we go home?"

The exploration is too much for us. We enjoy visiting ruins and appreciate the story each mountain has to tell. But Iron Mountain is too scarred, the ruins too visible. The environmental pain is still fresh.

We don't leave that place, we escape.

Iron Mountain   *August 12, 2012*

SUMMIT ELEVATION 2,726 feet

LOCATION AND DIRECTIONS Jackson. From Route 16 in Jackson, just north of the covered bridge and alongside the Wentworth Golf Course, turn west onto paved Green Hill Road. (From the point where the road turns to gravel, at 1.2 mi., it is called Iron Mountain Road.) At 1.4 mi. from Route 16, veer left onto Forest Road 119 (FR119) and continue steeply another 1.2 mi. to a small parking area just before the former Hayes Farm.

OUR ROUTE Iron Mountain Trail over summit and to ledges, up and back, with a side hike down to the Iron Mine ruins.

TRIP MILEAGE 3.4 miles round trip.

IF YOU GO The one thing Iron Mountain is known for is having some of the finest views of any mountain from its trailhead. Iron Mountain Road takes you up several hundred feet to the base of a wide farm pasture. The trail starts up through that pasture, offering magnificent views of the Presidentials toward Pinkham Notch.

One additional cautionary note: Iron Mountain road is steep and rough and may not be passable during the spring mud season and in winter.

| 12 |

Race to the Top

#12: Mount Cardigan

"Come on," I whisper, "you can take them. You're just as strong."

Ahead of us on the West Ridge Trail a pack of about ten teenagers and a couple adults lounge. They passed us about a quarter mile back, but we've caught up.

"They're teenagers," Janelle says. "They have a few years on me." I suspect she's more concerned about me trying to out-hike teenagers, but I let it go.

We are mid-way up Mt. Cardigan on a rare Wednesday hike. The weather is muggy and reports of a late afternoon storm have us hustling to do a one-out today up this relatively easy, but beautiful and exposed, mountain.

When they had passed us the first time, more than a few of them were sucking wind. "They're tired," I say. "Look at them. You have lots left in your gas tank."

"My what?"

"Never mind. Come on, let's blow by them."

We power up the trail and as we pass them, I work hard to control my heavy breathing. Janelle, however, barely seems to be exerting herself. The teens eye her warily, this ten-year-old with a pack and adult hiking boots gliding by them like she has wings.

"Told you," I say once we get out of earshot, triumphantly.

She's not as impressed. "They weren't moving. They'll catch up."

We wind up this historic mountain, energized from several days off. Cardigan is a popular mountain, its 3,155 feet low by White Mountain standards. But with a vast bald summit created by devastating forest fires in the 1850s, Cardigan feels much higher.

As we near the open ledges, we come across a series of mini waterfalls eroding down the trail and Janelle stops for some play time. The teenagers do catch up then, and rush by us. Janelle couldn't care less, though. The girl likes water. Pools. Ponds. Lakes. Ice. Water rushing down a trail. I slip off my pack and lean against a tree for some snacks and watch her fiddle in the mud, making tiny dams against rocks, pushing sticks this way and that.

I'm not a stickler for staying clean, and if the kid's happy rolling around in the dirt, as long as we are safe and warm, then bring on the filth.

After a bit, the now mud-caked girl and I break out onto the ledges, and I hear her take in a breath.

"It's like Monadnock!" she says. "Which way?"

Indeed. Someplace down below we zigged when we should have zagged, and we now find ourselves off trail by a hundred feet or so. There are no blazes or trail signs around us, but since I know the rest of the hike is above tree line and the day is clear, I just point and say, "Up!"

She's thrilled. She tackles the rock, grabbing with her hands and on her knees in some places. We are early in this journey, but her comfort zone on a mountain — above-treeline rock scrambling — is so clear it's a little frightening. I make a mental note to spend some time going over way-finding and compass skills.

For now, we are happy and free of trees. We explore the rocks wildly, moving ever upward, until the tip of the summit tower comes into view. We move down into a grassy crevasse, then pop out for good at the final long dome to the top.

Janelle pauses at a trail junction sign, the tower at her back and a stiff wind whipping through her hair. She looks at me and grins and my heart leaps because I understand what she feels and feel it as well.

Tough Cookie leans into the wind on the summit of Mount Cardigan.

Cardigan is extraordinary this day. Muggy, pre-storm clouds pile on top of each other in a dash up valley and the mountain mica glimmers in the ever-changing sunlight.

The teenagers who passed us have come and gone. They must have left down another trail.

We tuck in under the stairs of Cardigan's old fire tower to get out of the wind and settle back to people-watch. The summit is busy this day.

A group of girls not much older than Janelle, all from a nearby camp, is getting ready to leave, giggly and excited. One of them gives us a Hershey bar. A dad takes pictures of his daughter on a ledge; she wears a brightly colored tie-dye and twirls in the sun. Two dogs, a black poofy poodle and a tan and white terrier, run circles in a summit puddle, around and around, until water flies off them with every shake and soon they have everyone at the summit laughing. An older man with an ancient wide-brimmed hat and a canvas canteen stands back away from the crowd, looking off into the distance, smiling.

And so we lean our heads back against the weather-beaten concrete foundation and eat yogurt raisins and let time roll by, not a care in the world.

Mt. Cardigan   *August 16, 2012*

SUMMIT ELEVATION 3,155 feet

LOCATION AND DIRECTIONS Orange. Cardigan State Park can be reached
from several different directions. We climbed from the West Side, near
Orange. To get there, from Route 118, 0.5 mi. north of Canaan, turn right
(east) at a large state park sign. At 2.7 mi. from Route 118, bear right
just after crossing Orange Brook, then left at 3.4 mi. The parking area is
reached on another 0.7 mi. (or 4.1 mi. from Route 118). Restrooms and
maps are available at the picnic area. (Warning: Services are unavailable
during winter, and I assume the mountain road is not maintained.)

OUR ROUTE West Ridge Trail, up and back.

TRIP MILEAGE 3.0 miles round trip.

IF YOU GO There's nothing quite like Mt. Cardigan at any time of year.
At Cardigan Lodge, located at the eastern foot of the mountain, the
Appalachian Mountain Club sponsors all manner of programs for
families, beginners, and the more experienced. Pick a trail length,
prepare for the weather, and bring the family. Looking for the best
mountain to begin your quest? We suggest Cardigan.

| 13 |

Sharing the Forest

We are awash in blueberry bushes.

Blueberry Mountain lives up to its name: there are thousands of bushes in every direction, as far as the eye can see. We walk through slight paths along the ledges, carved between and around blueberry patches. To our east, Mount Moosilauke rises up, a monstrous shadow against our pretty little mountain.

Being here is a comforting respite after a disappointing start when Aaron, Janelle's brother, became sick at the trailhead and we all made the difficult decision to have Meena take him home. Today was to have been the first time we would have hiked with my wife and Janelle's brother. But here we are, on our own again.

It hasn't been easy finding hiking partners, mainly because our schedule has been so organic. Hiking in the Whites is rarely a predictable science. Plans often change at the last moment based on weather.

I watch Janelle, surefooted despite her blisters, and wonder how long it will be before she's able to out-hike us all, and finding friends to hike with will become even more difficult.

She stops in mid-step and freezes. "Whoa, look at that!"

A great pile of scat, tinged blue, sits in the middle of the trail. Whatever creature left this for us to discover was here just minutes ago.

"Is it a bear?" she asks. "What should we do?"

I have no idea what animal this is — another failing. Later we will

Awash in blueberry fields, Blueberry Mountain lives up to its name.

discover that it was coyote scat. But right now, I don't know. "Well," I say, "whatever it is pretty much gorged itself on blueberries, so I'm sure it's not interested in little girls."

She narrows her eyes and put her hands on her hips.

"Okay, okay, we'll take a picture and figure it out when we get down," I say quickly. "Until then, let's just talk and make noise while we walk so whatever it is knows we're here."

That makes her happy, and so time goes by as we tell stories and jokes. Blueberry Mountain Trail is a joy, an easy, rolling ledge walk surrounded by views and lookout ledges. We find the summit, which is mostly wooded, and settle in for lunch.

"So, do you remember what I told you about what to do if we see a bear?" I ask.

She nods. "Just move away slowly."

"Yes, and what if he charges?"

She thinks for a moment. "Well, don't run, because bears can run faster than you."

"Actually," I say using my straightest face, "if we're together, I can run."

She's confused. "Why?"

I shrug. "If a bear chases us, all I have to do is outrun *you*!"

Her eyes get wide and for a moment she's taken the bait, but I start to giggle and her shoulders relax. "You. Are. Mean!"

Later, as we approach the end of the trail, we once again come across a vast area of logging operations. Wide swaths of trees have been deforested and the trail runs right through a wide section of fallen timber and cut stumps.

"How can they do this?" Janelle asks. "It's right on the trail."

I explain that the White Mountains are a mixed-use forest, that logging is regulated and controlled here. "It used to be that whole wilderness areas could be cut down and left to erode," I say. "Now, at least, trees have to be replanted and logging is done in a less harmful way."

Sitting there among the tree shards and wide cuts, Janelle runs her fingertips over the stump of a small poplar. She's quiet and looks out over the long area that has been cut.

"See," I say, "because of the cut, we have great views up the valley."

She nods, but sadly. These aren't the views she wants, and if I am honest about it, I feel the same. But I leave her to her own thoughts about the value of the wilderness and our place in it. That's a nuanced topic, but here, among the sprawling clearcut, with a child who has only recently begun to comprehend her role in the natural world, the time for this discussion is not right.

For now, she can see only cut trees.

Blueberry Mountain   *August 19, 2012*

SUMMIT ELEVATION 2,662 feet

LOCATION AND DIRECTIONS Glencliff. To reach the eastern terminus of this trail, from Route 25 in Glencliff turn onto High Street and go 1.0 mi. to the south end of Long Pond Road (formerly known as the North and South Road). Trailhead parking is found on the left, 0.8 mi. up Long Pond Road. (Caution: Long Pond Road is rough in spots, and the road is closed during the winter months.)

OUR ROUTE Blueberry Mountain Trail (eastern terminus), up and back.

TRIP MILEAGE 3.4 miles round trip.

IF YOU GO At the time of this writing, there is extensive logging going on along Long Pond Road where the parking area to the trail is located.

There are no signs of any sort to indicate this is the road that leads to Blueberry Mtn. Trail. You can only find the trailhead by triangulating your location based on other nearby, signed, trailheads. The western terminus of the trail is located along Blueberry Mtn. Road in East Haverhill. This approach to Blueberry Mt. receives far less use than the Long Pond Road approach and as of this writing is also being impacted by an ongoing logging operation.

| 14 |

Let's See What This Kid Can Do

#14 & 15: Mounts Avalon and Willard

M t. Avalon juts sharply into Crawford Notch, a mountain between two mountains, nestled uncomfortably between Mount Willard's valley overlook and Mount Field's majestic height.

Our mountain is only 3,442 feet, but Avalon makes demands on a hiker. If we make it, Avalon's summit will be the highest Janelle has ever been, but she'll have to climb a relentlessly steep half mile to get there. And there's one more thing different about today. On this bright, clear, hot morning, my plan is to push Janelle further than she's ever been. Once we finish with Avalon, instead of returning to the comfort of the Appalachian Mountain Club's Highland Center, we'll come nearly all the way down, then turn right off the trail and push back up to Mount Willard.

Two in one day. Six and a half miles. It's the second day in a four-day run for us, and I don't know how she'll handle the extra miles, as well as the marathon hiking. So, as we sit in the parking lot, I take a little extra time taping her feet. Strangely, this little necessity has become something of a soothing ritual for us. She can do this herself, of course, but we like it this way. She enjoys the attention, and the extra ten minutes gives me a chance to gauge where her head is before we start.

If she has any doubts about the big day ahead, she doesn't let them show. And soon, she's bounding up the trail ahead of me, leaping up the steep rocks like she's been doing this all her life. All I can do is follow.

We reach the A–Z Trail junction and stop for a break.

"Where does that go?" Janelle asks, looking up the A–Z.

"To a bunch of places," I say. "Take that trail and we can go to Mount Tom or Field, or we can keep going all the way to Zealand Hut."

I see her puzzled expression. I have to remind myself how new the kid is to any of this, how even the concept of a wilderness hut is as foreign as another language.

"There are cabins in the mountains where hikers can go for water, or for a break, or even to stay overnight," I say.

"Like a hotel?" she asks.

"Kind of, a little more outdoorsy, with bunk beds and wooden tables, and during the colder times there's even a wood stove."

Her eyes get wide, excited. For some reason, Janelle is thrilled by towers or structures in the wild. As we prepared for this journey, we'd hike the Uncanoonucs in Goffstown, near our home. Those mountains are sprinkled with the ruins of former hotels and trams, and the echoes of centuries of tourists. Exploring "ghost houses," she would call it. "Can we go to a hut?" she asks.

"Of course," I say and make a mental note to add another destination to our ever-growing list.

The steep climb up to Avalon's sharp, small summit tires her, but the views more than compensate for the effort. Across the valley, Mount Webster's jagged cliffs shoot straight up out of Crawford Notch.

"Want to go over there this weekend?" I ask, pointing to Webster's summit.

"Sure!" she says without a moment's consideration.

I'm taken aback. "It's a hard hike, Mount Webster. Do you think you're ready for a mountain even higher than this one?"

She tilts her head in that way I'm getting used to seeing, a look that suggests that if I don't think she can do it, then why in heaven's name am I even asking. "It's on our list, right?"

I nod.

"Okay, then, sure." She goes back to her pistachios, the matter settled.

Janelle walks toward the light from the open summit of Mount Willard.

After lounging for half an hour on the warm Avalon rocks, we retrace our steps and meet our friend Steve half way down the mountain.

Steve is an old-school hiker, laid back, list-free and talkative. Our friend hikes for the sake of being in the woods, and Janelle takes to him immediately.

"Wow, she's a little rocket, isn't she?" Steve says to me at one point as Janelle barrels down trail ahead of us.

As it turns out, having Steve with us makes a difference. As we turn off the Avalon Trail and begin the second ascent of the day, Janelle begins to tire. Steve and I take turns encouraging her, keeping conversation going and her mind occupied.

Finally, at the long straightaway that leads to Mount Willard's summit, Janelle bolts ahead. A tunnel of trees leads to the open ledges overlooking the valley, and as the girl moves toward the light, she's surrounded by a halo of white sun, a little thing in the woods bathed in a glow.

We watch her reach the ledges. From here, a hiker can look straight down the heart of Crawford Notch. To the left, the steep walls of the southern Presidentials seem to shoot straight up from the road. There's no view like this, for the minimal amount of hiking, anywhere in the Whites.

She turns as we enter the summit area. "This is it!"

"Nice job," I say. "How do you feel?"

"Tired." But she's smiling.

We settle in for lunch, and hikers come and go. Willard is a busy and popular destination. Folks with full gear, tourists with nothing, and a variety of dogs visit.

After a salami sandwich and an apple, Janelle's energy returns and she turns to Steve. "Come on, Steve, let's see what's here!"

Beaten herd paths lead to various lookouts along Willard's cliff-like summit edge, and the girl is set on exploring them. I let the two of them get ahead of me. She's moving fast, with authority, and I'm struck by how solid her footing is becoming. She's developing trail legs, something she'll need in the weeks ahead as we set our sights on much longer and harder trails.

"Look, look!" she's shouting from somewhere ahead. I come around a turn expecting the two of them to be enjoying a grand view. There is a grand view, of course, but Janelle doesn't see it. Instead, she's crouched down, engaged in a staring contest with a deep green grasshopper.

She looks up at us and grins, and what can one do after a smile like that? Steve and I share a knowing look and sit down to watch the girl and the insect, the views forgotten.

Mts. Avalon and Willard   *August 20, 2012*

SUMMIT ELEVATIONS Mt. Avalon, 3,442 feet; Mt. Willard, 2,865 feet.

LOCATION AND DIRECTIONS Crawford Notch. Follow US Route 302 to the top of Crawford Notch and the old railroad depot on the south side of the highway. Park in either the small lot next to the depot, at the adjacent Highland Center, or in designated parking areas along Route 302.

OUR ROUTE Avalon Trail (located behind Crawford Depot) up and back, left on Mt. Willard Trail, up and back.

TOTAL MILEAGE 6.8 miles round trip.

IF YOU GO The AMC's Highland Center is a good jumping-off point for any number of adventures in Crawford Notch. For Avalon and/or Willard, park near the old Crawford Notch train station. Avalon is a steep hike for the miles, but if you want a quick beginner hike with magnificent views, Willard should be it.

| 15 |

Take Two

#16: Cherry Mountain (Mt. Martha)

Two weeks ago, we attempted to hike Cherry Mountain up to its Mount Martha summit. We didn't make it. I had pushed Janelle too far, too many hikes in a row, too much pressure perhaps. A half mile up the mellow trail, she turned to me with tears in her eyes and asked if we could go home.

I crouched down to be face to face with her. "What's the matter, kid-o?"

She couldn't answer. She shook her head. She looked miserable. We turned around.

On the way down she said she felt bad for disappointing me.

"For what?" I asked, honestly perplexed.

"For not being able to do it."

"No, no," I tried to comfort her. "I'm proud of you for making a tough decision, an adult decision. The mountain will be here waiting for us when we decide to come back."

So now we have returned. The day is hot. Her feet are beat up. Yesterday she hiked the longest hike of her life. And as we turn to face down the mountain that turned us back once, I wonder how she'll handle the hike this time.

I stop her at the trailhead, and once again crouch to her eye level.

"Here we are again," I say. "Are you okay?"

She nods. "I'm fine."

"You'd tell me if you weren't?"

She looks at me with impatience. "I'm fine! Let's go."

Mount Martha is not a difficult hike, and it is uneventful. The mellow carriage trail leads up, up, up, moderately, but ever on an incline. The Cherry Mountain Trail wears on a hiker.

But today, Janelle is fierce. After yesterday's successful long hike, and understanding that Cherry has thus far been the only mountain that turned her back, she storms the trail.

For the first time in our hiking journey, I say two words to her that I hoped to put off saying until much, much later. "Wait up!"

We reach the summit (her new high point) in record time, and are thrilled to find a meadow. This is new for her. August goldenrod and wild flowers cover the summit, while a small clearing and fire pit provide a pleasant lunch spot.

"This is the summit?" she asks. "There are flowers here. It's a field."

"Is that a bad thing?" I ask.

"No, no! It's wonderful!"

We explore the summit, finding viewpoints here and there. An obvious footpath next to the foundations of the former fire tower leads us to a westerly lookout. Wildflowers taller than the girl, filled with grasshoppers and bees, force us to be a bit careful, but Martha's summit makes up for the dreary ascent.

There are few summits that offer a better view of Mt. Washington and the Northern Presidentials, but there in the wildflowers, surrounded by light and color, Janelle isn't very interested in distant views. We are filled with sensation right here. Why look across the valley?

After a while, Janelle says, "Why would anyone do that?" She's looking at the fire pit.

"What, build a fire?"

"No, cigarettes. There are cigarette butts in there."

I hadn't even noticed.

"You hike all the way up here, in the forest, and then you smoke?" She pauses. "And then you litter?"

Ten-year-old righteous indignation can be a funny thing, but I maintain a serious look. I'm glad that somewhere along the way, in her exposure to exercise and nature, she has drawn the conclusion that smoking is bad. Or at least littering is bad.

But then she surprises me by taking action.

"Only one thing to do," she says. She pulls an empty snack baggie from her pack and slips her hand into it. "My uncle John taught me how to pick up dog poop like this."

She delicately picks up each cigarette butt, wraps the baggy up and around them and closes the strip. She slips the bag back into her pack, brushes off her hands and goes back to her juice.

Not once in the decades I have been hiking, I think to myself, have I ever picked up a cigarette butt. Not once. I'm horrified at myself. I eat the rest of my lunch quietly, making sure to properly dispose of all my wrappers.

Mt. Martha *August 21, 2012*

SUMMIT ELEVATION 3,573 feet

LOCATION AND DIRECTIONS Twin Mountain. From Route 3 north of Twin Mountain village, turn onto Route 115 and continue 1.9 mi. to the trailhead parking lot on the right side of the highway..

OUR ROUTE Cherry Mountain Trail (located directly across from Lennon Road) up and back.

TRIP MILEAGE 3.8 miles round trip.

IF YOU GO Cherry Mountain has two summits, both equally worthy of exploration. The other summit, Owl's Head, can be reached either by continuing on for about a mile from the summit of Martha, or as a separate hike up the Owl's Head Trail, from a footpath found a few miles further along Route 115.

Note: Besides our western approach up Cherry Mountain, there's also an eastern approach that leads to the summit of Mt. Martha from Cherry Mountain Road near Bretton Woods. It's actually an extension of the trail we used to ascend the mountain and goes by the same name. The Cherry Mountain Road approach is about twice as long as the Route 115 approach, and receives far less use than its western counterpart.

Gear 101: Finding It, Using It, Breaking It

Finding the proper gear for a nine- or ten-year-old to climb big mountains in all manner of weather is a race against time and public opinion.

Time because in the year or so that Janelle has been hiking seriously her foot size changed from 5 to 6 and now nearly 6½. Near the end, her arms were popping out of base layers that just months ago she seemed to fit fine in. And don't even get started on the fashion of mountain gear for a ten-year-old girl. (Pink is ok, but not girly pink. Flower patterns are cool, but not pastels and only on certain items of clothing!)

And public opinion because the concept of buying a real pack, or non-fashion North Face is clearly not high on the list of gear retailers. Early in our quest, Janelle and I walked into a well-known outdoor retailer and asked about day-packs for kids.

"Well, what will she be using it for," the skeptical clerk asked looking at Tough Cookie.

"Hiking," I said.

Silence.

"Hiking mountains," I tried again. "The White Mountains."

"We don't have anything that small for that," he said after a long pause.

That's not to say such gear isn't made. It is. But other than Hello Kitty box store backpacks for school, finding her safe, comfortable and appropriate hiking gear has been a trial. Perhaps it's different in Colorado or Oregon, but the New England commercial market for good kids gear is pretty slim pickings.

We were lucky in two ways. One, Meena was only a bit bigger than Janelle when we started. Now, Janelle is a bit bigger than Meena. But much of the everyday gear Janelle uses is hand-me-downs from Meena.

The second way was a glorious box of mountain gear we found along the side of the road in Bethlehem. Trail shoes. Base layers. Fleece and hats. It was all there, it all fit, and Janelle wore it non-stop from that point on, and continues to wear them today.

So, if you don't have a wife who is the same size as your hiking child, and you haven't come across some gear sitting along the side of the road, here's some suggestions to get your kid the goods and make sure they get the best use of their gear:

Hand me downs: Ask folks like me. That's what we did. There are hiking kids out there, mostly the sons and daughters of other hikers. Go to the hiking forums and ask. Check Craig's List regularly. Like most kids' clothes, hiking gear lasts a season and it's done. Those parents likely got the gear from somebody else's kid, and now it can be yours.

Kids are tough: Remember, your kid is much tougher than you. Do they need Gore-Tex or can they get by fine with a lesser brand. Janelle hiked her Walmart trail shoes into the dirt and they kept her warm and safe the whole journey. With kids, the fit is often more important than the brand. If their feet are blister-free, their hands warm, and the pack comfortable, they likely won't need a $500 Deuter.

They can use adult gear: Janelle was ten when we did this, she wasn't and isn't a baby. Treat your hiking kid like a baby and your hike will fail. You have "adult" water bottles, stuff sacks, first aid kits, whistles and maps. Teach them how to use them and let them use them. Carrying a Nalgene water bottle while your child carries a cheap cartoon squirt bottle will irritate them. If they really want to make the gear their own, let them paint or sticker up that water bottle. Just remember, they are climbing adult mountains, give them adult resources to accomplish that task.

Let them try stuff on and walk around the house in it before they get on the trail: Before our overnighter, we laid her sleeping bag out on the floor of the kitchen and made her get in it. Then, we taught her how to put it into a stuff sack. Everything from tying boot laces to extending poles to packing a pack. Do it at home first.

Learn how to take care of it: We have a gear area in our basement where all our hiking and running clothes and gear are stored. After a hike, we march straight into the basement (where the washing machine also is) and clean and store our gear. Like any of their other possessions, teach them to respect the gear.

They will break things: They will. Janelle broke two hiking poles and lost a glove. Big deal. If they are using the gear correctly, eventually, it will break. You break things too.

| 16 |

Higher and Higher

#17: Mount Webster

We inch down toward Silver Cascade Brook. The Webster-Jackson Trail diverges just before the brook, and in order to continue climbing up to Mount Webster we must first descend steeply.

"How am I supposed to do this?" Janelle asks.

For a couple dozen feet, our trail drops down amid huge rocks, roots and gravel. The route is tricky for someone with long legs and trail experience. For her, down climbing on such tough terrain can be crippling.

"Toss your poles; use your hands or even your butt," I say. I'm below her. When traversing sections like this, I get ahead and watch her come down. I figure at least from in front I have a better chance of catching her if she falls.

"Toss my poles?" she says.

Throwing gear on the ground ahead, or just throwing gear, is thankfully not something that happens in real life. Like peeing in the woods, burping, or blowing your nose in a hiking manner known as "blowing snot rockets," tossing poles is foreign to her. We've come to refer to hiking practices as "on-the-trail behavior."

"Just throw them down, and pick them up later," I say. "It frees up your hands so you can climb down."

She does, and free of her poles and her inhibitions, she scrambles down easily. As she goes to collect her poles, she sees the falls and it's like Janelle is caught in headlights. "Whoa!"

Celebrating the view from ledges near the summit of Mount Webster.

Cascade Brook pools here, at the bottom of a small falls. Thin, ribbon-like veins of water slide this way and that down a beautiful moss-encrusted rock face into a deep and clear swimming hole. The trail swings us down and directly in front of the pool. It is a magical place.

Janelle dawdles, taking unusually long to cross, her attention sharply drawn to the gleaming pool.

"Would you like to take a break here?" I ask.

"Yes!" she shouts. She realizes she's been found out and smiles.

And so we sit, not even halfway through our hike, and fulfill a promise we made to each other months earlier. If we wish to stop, we stop. If we wish to explore, we explore. There's no hurry. There's no agenda. Every mushroom, waterfall, slug and leaf is as important as the summit.

A couple hikers pass us by and ask me if I'd like my picture taken with my daughter. If Janelle hears this, she doesn't say anything, and I am too selfish to correct them. We get in position with the waterfall behind us and I crouch down to be at equal height with my partner. And as the picture is taken, Janelle puts her arm on my shoulder for balance and I feel a moment's regret that she is not my daughter, that there is not that bond between us. But we are here, together, and she is happy, the sun is shining, and today, for once, her feet don't hurt. So, I'll take it.

The push to the summit is uneventful, but the summit itself is magnificent. Webster's summit rests at the edge of the Presidential Range and towers over Crawford Notch. Across the notch, I point out Mount Willard and we watch as a tourist train chugs past far below. Webster is nearly a 4,000-footer and this is the highest she's ever been.

Today is the last hike in a four-day string and we chat a bit about the challenges of hiking every day. "I don't mind getting up early," Janelle says. "I could hike every day."

Incredibly, like out of a movie, we hear footsteps approaching.

"Hey, what's for lunch?" Janelle and I turn from our summit perch and watch as a big, middle-aged hiker with a scruffy pack and both knees wrapped hauls himself up near our rock. The summit of Webster is on the Appalachian Trail and he looks like a thru-hiker.

"Well," I begin, "today's menu is PB&J, pineapple juice and carrots."

"Sounds great!" he says. "Mind if I join you? I don't want to bother you two in the middle of lunch."

We don't mind at all. In fact, we've begun to look forward to the company of other hikers, especially upbeat and cheerful ones like this fellow.

His trail name is Rain Man, and it turns out he's section hiking. He's been on the trail through New Hampshire for a week and is going to cap off this part of his AT hike by finishing atop Mount Washington.

We sit and chat amicably. Well, he does most of the talking, actually. He's from Tennessee. He tells us about his AT journey so far, and talks proudly about his daughter, who thru-hiked the trail in one shot a couple years ago. "Guess you could say I'm following in her footsteps, just more slowly," he says, and laughs.

Janelle sits quietly through most of this, but now speaks up. "What's a thru-hiker?" she asks.

I think of the 2,000-plus mile AT and the effort, time and determination required to hike that long-distance trail. I look into Janelle's eyes and think, *uh-oh.*

Mt. Webster

SUMMIT ELEVATION 3,910 feet

LOCATION AND DIRECTIONS Crawford Notch, Trailhead parking is found along Route 302 just a short distance above the "Gateway" entrance to the Notch. The good-sized lot is found on the south, or railroad track, side of the highway, several hundred yards east of AMC's Highland Center and the refurbished train depot.

OUR ROUTE Webster-Jackson Trail (Webster Branch) up and back. Trailhead is located just north of Elephant Head on the west side of 302 near Crawford Depot.

TRIP MILEAGE 4.8 miles round trip.

IF YOU GO A fine loop can be made over Mts. Webster and Jackson by continuing on from either summit via the Webster Cliff Trail. On our hike, we also stopped at an overlook called Bugle Cliff. Both Bugle Cliff and Elephant Head overlook can be reached via short hikes along the Webster-Jackson Trail, and both are well worth your time and energy. Be careful of ice in the winter, though, as both overlooks are steep.

It's Raining Toads

#18: Mount Roberts

J anelle is showing off.

Meena and I hang back to watch her motor over the wide, warm ledges up Mount Roberts. Having my wife with us improves everyone's mood. Janelle adores her, and the kid clearly wants to illustrate how strong she's become.

Not that the Mt. Roberts Trail is difficult. Despite its ease, this obscure mountain in the Ossipee Range near Lake Winnipesaukee is turning into one of our favorites.

The trails here are wide, well-marked and moderate, and after about an hour of easy hiking we begin to bask in views back to the lake and beyond. We can't hike Mount Roberts without running into the area's centerpeice, the 5,500-acre mountaintop estate known as Castle in the Clouds. The three of us stop near an open ridge to consider the sprawling property, which can be seen from several lookouts along the trail.

Shoes built that property, and today it's a popular tourist destination. Millionaire shoe manufacturer Thomas Gustave Plant built the estate for his second wife, ruthlessly buying land in the area and using the structures on the bought property to build his own grand mansion.

At the time, in 1913 and 1914, the Craftsman-style house was a picture of modernity with its circular shower and interlocking tiles. Today, the look is dated, but there's no denying the location is superb.

Tough Cookie and Short Step (Meena) pause to check out the view on the way up Mount Roberts.

"Is that the castle?" Janelle asks.

Her grandparents took her and her brother there when they were little, and the trip left an impression on her. It's easy to understand why—the upper Lakes Region is beautiful. Plant's castle tucks into an outcropping formerly known as the Crow's Nest. From our bird's-eye view, we watch a tourist bus run guests to the front entrance and can see plenty of visitors milling about the parking area and abundant trails.

We stroll ever up, the two ladies chatting, and I feel my shoulders relax, my steps fall lightly.

Near the summit, we come as close to a moose as we have so far. A still-steaming mound of moose scat piles up in the trail, right next to a freshly trampled moose bed in high grass just off the trail. It is as if the moose heard us coming and slipped away five minutes ago.

"Is it still here?" Janelle asks, a mixture of hope and terror in her voice. She has never seen a moose, and would gladly sacrifice her lunch for the chance.

"It's still close, kid-o," I say, "but, it's safe to say it knows we're here."

"Here, moose, moose, moose," Meena calls. Janelle joins in and soon the two ladies in my life are shrieking into the woods, laughing, and whistling for Mr. Moose to join our hike.

Later, after spending a long lunch at the summit, Meena begins the task of teaching Janelle to become a catcher of toads.

It's not as easy as you'd think. Those little guys can be fast. Plus, you have to ignore the clear, oily liquid that ends up in your hand. In other words, toads have a propensity for urinating on you when handled. And contrary to mythological belief, you cannot get warts from toads. Though there is a toxin located just behind the toad's eyes that can irritate your mouth and make you nauseous if you try to eat one.

Don't try to eat one.

Our hike today has been all about toads. They are everywhere, tiny little creatures bounding this way and that over the trail, rustling in the leaves and, yes, peeing on our hands.

Perhaps Mount Roberts' deep oak forest offers toads cover from predatory birds. Perhaps the surrounding area's wetlands breed plentiful mosquito bounty for toads to eat. Either way, there are so many, we begin to count. Ten. Eighteen. Twenty-four. Thirty-five. Forty. Fifty.

Then, just as we are about to leave the trail at the end of the day, we see one final toad. Fifty-Two.

We all laugh. It's a sign, of course. The Toad Gods have honored our adventure by providing us the same number of toads as mountains in our quest.

Perfect. Delightful. Despite the pee.

Mt. Roberts   *August 24, 2012*

SUMMIT ELEVATION 2,582 feet

LOCATION AND DIRECTIONS From Route 25 in Moultonborough, take
    Route 109 south to its intersection with Route 171. Continue south
    on Route 171 to Ossipee Park Road and the entrance to Castle in the
    Clouds. The trailhead is found at the very end of Ossipee Park Road.

OUR ROUTE Mt. Roberts Trail (located north of the salmon pond, past the
    barn) up and back.

TRIP MILEAGE 5.0 miles round trip.

IF YOU GO One great highlight of this mountain and this trail is the area
    around the trailhead itself. Located in a sweeping farm field, just over a

small ridge from Castle in the Clouds, the trailhead offers a variety of attractions from a salmon pond to an ice cream stand. There are picnic benches and a variety of smaller trails. And best of all, for a quarter, you can get fish food and whittle the day away feeding the rainbow trout.

| 18 |

Mud and Snakes

#19: Mount Success

"I'm stuck!" Janelle wails.

Her predicament strikes me as funny; she's standing in the rain, up to her calves in mud. Both her feet are submerged in the thick, swirling mud between two wooden plank bridges. I imagine her feet are cold.

We are nearly two miles up the Success Trail and everything is wet. Despite a forecast that called for warm, clear skies, the heavens opened up on us thirty minutes ago, and it's still drizzling. Now, Tough Cookie is stuck. She can't move her feet, and she sways back and forth, trying to figure out some means of extraction.

She senses my amusement and it irritates her. "No, really, I can't move!"

There's a hint of desperation in her voice, so I find some solid ground to brace myself, reach under her armpits and lift her out of the muck. She breaks free with a squishy pop.

And so we stand there, looking at her feet, which are solidly encased in an impenetrable layer of goo. It really is funny, but I hold my tongue.

"What do we do now?" she asks.

"Well, we can turn around if you got really wet, or just kick off some of that mud and let's keep going."

Given the option of turning around, she wavers. She needs to begin

Mount Success turns into a wet, muddy trial of a hike.

making these kinds of decisions for herself, judging on her own how uncomfortable is too uncomfortable.

"Ugh, it's gross," she grumbles, and I know she's decided to keep going.

Her trail runners appear ruined. Last weekend, as we prepared for our hike up Blueberry, we came across a pile of boxes on the side of the road with a "free" sign propped against them. We struck gold: piles of tech wear and down jackets, many in kids' or small women's sizes, filled the boxes. We took home jackets, base layers, hats and fleece neck warmers. The gear was a few years old but not damaged in any way. It was as though a hiking guardian angel had dropped a pile of hiking gear for Janelle to use, free, unworn and fitting her perfectly. And in that stack we found a brand new pair of Faded Glory trail shoes. They fit her perfectly.

Considering they were a Walmart brand, we saw them as nothing more than a good alternative for warm, rainy, muddy days when we didn't want her to wear out better boots. And now, on her first hike with the "new" shoes, they appear wrecked.

The drizzle continues as we make our way past the Appalachian Trail boundary signs, and once again Janelle and I chat about thru-hiking.

"That's nuts," she says upon hearing the AT is more than 2,000 miles long. "Who does that?"

I tuck those words away to use as ammunition when the day comes when she decides to do it herself.

We breach treeline and the weather holds long enough for us to spend ten minutes at Mount Success's flat open summit. The Mahoosuc Range spreads out around us, and along with it some of the most difficult hiking along the AT. A warm but vicious wind roars over the summit, and before long a pile of storm clouds begin to form to the north.

We head down quickly and are passed by another thru-hiker heading toward Maine. Janelle watches him pass, and only smiles when he says "hi." We hike by some old logging equipment, old bent log sleds and broken rails. And on the short side path to some nearby ledges, we find a beaten, ancient bucket.

Finally, we break out onto some cliff ledges with a view back of the Success summit, and as the girl leads the way over the warm, wet rocks she steps right over an enormous, coiled garter snake. It is the largest of its kind I have ever seen, but it appears just as surprised by the girl's intrusion as I am by the snake's presence.

"Ah!" I say, as the beautiful snake, shimmering in moisture, uncoils and slithers away.

Janelle turns too late. The snake is gone.

"Did you see it?" I ask.

"See what?" she says.

"A snake, a garter snake. You just stepped right over it!"

"What? Oh man! I missed it!"

She's sad she missed it, but I can't shake the image of her little bare legs stepping right over a snake. I'm irritated at myself for not seeing it in her path, but thankful that it wasn't a more dangerous reptile. This time.

Mt. Success
August 31, 2012

SUMMIT ELEVATION 3,565 feet

LOCATION AND DIRECTIONS Unincorporated town of Success. From the center of Berlin on Route 16, cross the Mason Street Bridge to the east side of the Androscoggin River and Hutchins Street, and then to Success Pond Road. The trailhead is about 5.4 miles from the beginning of Success Pond Road and there is limited parking space on the right side of the infamously rough gravel road.

OUR ROUTE Success Trail up and back.

TRIP MILEAGE 6.3 miles round trip (includes the 0.3-mile loop to lookout ledges).

IF YOU GO A primary challenge of reaching Mt. Success is not the trail itself but the road you need to drive on to get there. Success Pond Road is a dreadful, and well used, logging road. Cars without high clearance will have problems. And if the road itself isn't enough to challenge your nerves, the huge, fast-moving logging trucks that still use the road will raise your blood pressure and have you white-knuckling the drive to the trailhead. Finally, though Success Pond Road is open in winter, it is not maintained.

| 19 |

Look, Canada!

#20: Magalloway Mountain

I'm irritated the moment we finally pull into the trailhead parking lot.

First, we are nearly ten miles of logging road off any main road and only a couple miles away from Canada. So what are all these cars doing here?

Second, do any of these people understand trailhead etiquette? A half dozen of the cars are parked horizontally, cutting off spaces and making latecomers like ourselves struggle to find space.

I wish this weren't so, because the logging road ride to this place is nothing short of spectacular, through some wonderful fir forest, tablelands and rolling hills of far northern New Hampshire.

Magalloway Mountain is, by far, our northernmost target. It took us two hours from Whitefield to get here, but the day is warm and clear and a slight breeze keeps bugs away. Even better, Janelle and I are thrilled that Meena will be hiking with us for the weekend.

The parking area sits above 2,500 feet, meaning a hiker only has to hike about one mile of trail with 800 feet of elevation gain. The Coot Trail is relentless, climbing hard immediately, but all three of us are feeling strong and eager to check out the tower area at the summit. The trail is an old carriage road, but rubber erosion bars have begun to slip and now gravel trenches twist this way and that in some areas. Still, a hiker can't get lost here.

We are surprised by how many people are on the trail. And it gets

Meena and Janelle approach
the summit tower atop
Mount Magalloway.

worse after about an hour when we do reach the summit area. There
are dozens of people at the summit. The farthest mountain on our list
turns out to be the most crowded.

Meena and Janelle are all grins, embracing the crowd like it's a
party. And after a moment of disappointment I begin to see their
point. Families with little ones crawl like ants over and up the tall fire
tower. The various viewpoints are stacked with people waiting to get
a glimpse of the amazing Great North Woods. Dogs trot this way and
that playfully. Picnic tables overflow with baskets of lunchables.

There's a ranger cabin with an enormous rain water tank attached
to the gutter. A message on the side of the tank, written in black pen,
reads, "Danger — check for mice in barrel — not for drinking."

Before tackling the fire tower, we hike down to a viewing bench
overlooking a cliff—the east side of the mountain simply drops off
down to the valley below. When our turn comes, we break out our
own lunch of salami, juice and carrots and eat while hummingbirds

buzz in the trees around us. The wooden bench sits two, and the ladies take up position and chat amicably. We are all surprised by Magalloway's wonderful summit.

Families come and go, and little kids no older than 2 or 3 hustle about, their parents warning them of the steep drop-offs.

After a bit, we wander back to the fire tower and are surprised to discover tourists and hikers from Manchester, Goffstown and Bedford all staked out at the top. The 37-foot tower is one of the oldest lookout spots in the state. The original tower was built in 1910; the current one was constructed in the 1960s. The tower is still used for fire spotting, but the cab is closed this weekend.

"There's a lot of kids here," Janelle says, leaning over the railing near the top of the tower. We look down at the families and little ones. "I really like it here."

We take pictures and climb down but are unwilling to leave just yet. So the three of us lay out our remaining food and picnic at the base of the tower. We meet an Australian dad whose smallest child, a girl of maybe two, is climbing the tower stairs. Her mom hovers over her, as the child's hands can barely reach each rung. But the tiny hiker fights her way up to the top, and folks nearby stop to watch. When the baby reaches the top, her mom picks her up and we all cheer.

The day passes. The North Country is good to us.

"You know," I say, "we're only a couple miles from the border of Canada."

"I've never been in another country," Janelle says.

We both look at Meena, who sighs and says, "Let's go to Canada!"

Magalloway Mtn.   *September 1, 2012*

SUMMIT ELEVATION 3,383 feet

LOCATION AND DIRECTIONS Pittsburg. Follow Route 3 North well past
   Pittsburg's town center to near mile marker 235 and gravel Magalloway
   Road. After crossing the Connecticut River and bearing left twice (at
   2.3 and 2.9 mi.), turn right onto the access road at 5.3 miles and continue
   another 3.1 mi. to the trailhead.

OUR ROUTE Coot Trail, up and back.

TRIP MILEAGE 2.0 miles round trip (slightly more if you decide to take
Bobcat Trail one way, or explore the various summit lookouts).

IF YOU GO The hike to Magalloway Mtn. from the trailhead, though steep, is
short and well-marked and should be an easy hike any time of the year.
However, Magalloway Road is another story. The private road, which
sees year-round logging traffic, may be gated in winter and closed to
motor vehicle use by the public.

Smuggling a Ten-Year-Old into Canada, Many Times

"Look, I'm in Canada," Janelle shouts. "Now I'm not. Now I am!"

We are hiking the border of Canada and the United States toward Fourth Connecticut Lake, the headwaters of the mighty river of the same name. We've already hiked Mt. Magalloway and it's late in the day, but there is something dreamlike and giddy about being here that keeps us motivated and excited.

The Fourth Connecticut Trail to the headwaters is short, just over 1.5 miles, but begins with a steep, rocky climb up above the border station at the top of New Hampshire. This is unusual for us, a welcome change of pace here among the French *no trespassing* signs and metal post markers in the middle of the trail.

In a moment of inspired levity, Meena lies down on the United States side of a post while Janelle does the same on the Canadian side and I snap of picture of the two ladies in two different countries, yet cheek to cheek at the same time.

We reach the lake, but in early September the headwaters of the longest and largest river in New England is today just a marshy swamp, really little more than a wetland. According to the Nature Conservancy, which maintains the area, the 2.5-acre lake is actually a northern acidic mountain tarn.

We stand at the shore and look out onto the bog grass and try to imagine that this little splotch of wet will make its way down through the North Country, form the border between New Hampshire and Vermont, then provide riverfront to Springfield and Hartford before dumping into a sandbar in Long Island Sound, some 407 miles south of where we stand.

"This is it?" Janelle asks.

"Yup."

We snack, and chat, and relax on a stump near the shore where I mix up

Meena and Janelle, cheek to cheek, yet in two different countries on the border trail to Fourth Connecticut Lake.

peanut butter pretzels for cheese pretzels and for some reason Janelle and Meena find my broken taste buds to be hilarious.

The real joy of this hike though is the trail itself, and on the way back with the sun behind us and high on the ridge between the two countries we have a straight shot view into Canada as we hike through thick balsam fir and red spruce.

We climb back down to the border station and horse around the various flags and obelisks that mark the border. In the meantime, the bored border patrol officer eyes us with amusement. We have more hiking to do tomorrow and a long drive home. But none of us really want to leave this place, almost another world, alone at the top of our home state.

"I've never been to another country," Janelle says as we make our way home down the empty Route 3.

"Do you feel any different," I ask.

She smiles and shakes her head and looks wistfully out the window into the northern forest.

| 20 |

Kingdom of the Locusts

#21: Sugarloaf Mountain (Groveton)

It takes a lot to rip up Carhartts, but the young man we meet on the trail has Carhartt pants that are torn to pieces. He wears a T-shirt that says, "Yes, as a matter of fact, I *was* born in a barn." He carries one plastic bottle of water. His feet are clad in sneakers.

He's a North Country boy out for a quick run up the very, very steep flank of Sugarloaf Mountain in Groveton, and as he passes us on his way down he seems amused. Here we are, three city slickers, in our engineered gear and hiking poles, huffing and puffing our way up his mountain.

"You're almost there," he says softly, almost shyly. "There's a wildflower field of, um, well, I'm not sure of what flowers they are, but once you pass through that it gets less steep."

We've been tramping around the North Country these past few days and have very much enjoyed meeting locals like this young man who tend to seem genuinely curious about why we're here, in Nash Stream Forest, and not following the conga line up Franconia Notch or some other equally beautiful but tourist-heavy hiking locale.

He tells us about how, in the winter, he and his friends drive their snowmobiles up this trail. "Well, we try, anyway," he says. "Sometimes we don't make it."

We watch in wonder as he heads down, sure-footed and fast.

"Snowmobiles up this trail, huh?" Janelle says.

Meena shrugs. "North Country boys at play!"

Nash Stream Forest is a sadly overlooked area of woodland in Groveton and Stark. Nash Stream is the home of the Cohos Trail, the state's only long-distance hiking trail. Unlike the party on Magalloway yesterday, today we have Sugarloaf Mountain nearly to ourselves.

The trail is poorly marked and overgrown. The incline is relentless, giving us almost no flat hiking in the full 2.2-mile length to the summit.

Earlier, Meena and Janelle sprang into action to save a fuzzy yellow and black caterpillar from being squashed by an oncoming car roaring down the dirt road near our trailhead. Now, as we reach the clearing the Carhartts boy spoke of, we enter the kingdom of the locusts. The old warden's cabin clearing is saturated with tall grass and goldenrod, and locusts swirl this way and that, a spinning mass of insects leaping on our clothes and under and over us. Janelle stands amid the grass and holds out her arms, and bright green and yellow insects swarm onto her hands and shoulders

Finding joy in such an amazing place is easy, but we don't laugh, as doing so might get us a mouthful of the creatures.

The cabin was left to return to the earth when the tower above was dismantled, and now rubble is all that remains: cement blocks, tin roofs and wood. Janelle slowly picks through the refuse, fascinated. The girl loves ruins. Coming upon an old wall or cellar hole brightens her up and often threatens to derail an entire hike. I've grown used to these explorations, but Meena tilts her head at me as Janelle steps near an old foundation.

I shrug. "She's like you," I say. "She likes falling-down buildings."

Meena laughs, Meena who has pulled us off the highway to explore millyard ruins on the horizon. "Sounds good," she says.

After a while, we break through the overgrowth, regain the trail and jog the final tenth of a mile to the summit, which is small and the only above-treeline spot of the hike. But it is remarkable, offering us nearly 360-degree views of the surrounding North Country.

Directly below us, we can see the full expanse of the 200-acre Nash Stream Bog. The bog was Nash Pond until its dam broke in the late 1960s and it emptied into the valley. On the horizon, wind turbines

Less-visited Sugarloaf Mountain near Nash Stream offers up one of the finest summit views of our journey.

in Milan spin slowly, and to the south, the Percys pierce the blue sky, their open ledges a beacon.

"Hey kid-o," I say, pointing to North Percy. "Tomorrow."

"Awesome!"

If we had the whole day, we would spend it atop Sugarloaf. Janelle and Meena collect old nails and colorful glass and build their own little tower at the site of the old structure. Janelle takes a picture of me with my wife near the old summit sign, carved with the initials of countless hikers before us.

The day is ours. The mountain offers us warmth and calm this day. I sit with my two favorite ladies and close my eyes to the sun, allowing the sound of locusts and the rustle of the wind to bring me peace.

Sugarloaf Mountain

September 2, 2012

SUMMIT ELEVATION 3,710 feet

LOCATION AND DIRECTIONS From Route 3 in Groveton, take Route 110 East 2.6 mi. to Emerson Road (on the left). Follow Emerson Road for 2.2 mi. and turn onto Nash Stream Road. The trailhead is reached in 8.3 mi., about 60 yards past a bridge over Nash Stream.

OUR ROUTE Sugarloaf Mountain Trail up and back.

TRIP MILEAGE 4.4 miles round trip.

IF YOU GO Be warned: The trailhead is poorly signed. As noted above, look for the bridge over Nash Stream a little more than eight miles from the start of Nash Stream Road. Parking is available on either side of bridge. The trailhead can be found by walking past the south side of a cabin just off the road on your left. Also, Nash Stream Road is not open to motor vehicle traffic in winter and is used mainly as a snowmobile route.

| 21 |

Getting Our Heads Around It

| #22: North Percy |

The promise of views is often the fuel that propels us up a difficult pitch or gives us the incentive to navigate a tough stream crossing or muddy bog.

Today is not one of those days.

We are only a mile up the Percy Peaks Trail, and Tough Cookie is faltering. This hike is our fourth in a row, Labor Day, and we have pushed hard this past weekend. We're on our final climb, North Percy, one of the most beautiful on our list, but we're both beat.

Janelle is having a hard time shaking the images out of her head of all her friends playing at home, enjoying this day off from school. But unlike at Mount Martha last month, there are no tears and no drama. Yet.

She just drags, and that at least is progress. I'm proud that she forges on, that she understands that this hike, this time, is about mental discipline and determination. Someday, she may need to rely on those traits.

But, despite our tired legs, we fight back. We make up a head game called "What I'd rather be doing." I start.

"I'd rather be eating a popsicle than hiking!" I proclaim. Then, we hike for ten minutes while she thinks of something to add.

After the allotted time, she shouts, "I'd rather be eating a popsicle and hanging out with my friends than hiking!"

And so it goes. We wind up this beautiful and steep mountain, past the enormous moss-covered rock slabs, past the thick pine overgrowth, onto the rich ridge and finally up into the azure sky, our legs becoming strong, our hearts pounding in our ears, together.

All the while, we proclaim our deepest desires to be someplace else.

Just before the col between North and South Percy, she slips on a particularly tricky scramble and goes down hard, her knee banging a jutting rock. She stays down for a long moment before I finally slip off my pack and bend down next to her. She's fighting back tears.

"Ouch," I say softly, "that was a bad one, huh?"

There's a red mark, just below her knee, the skin bruised.

"Can you bend your knee, move your toes?"

I understand this moment to be a watershed for her, enough of an injury to turn her around and send her home. She's fighting for the strength to go forward, to forge on. But this time, this one, hurts.

"OK," I say, "we're going to have to deal with this. Come on, sit on that rock."

She obeys and I pull out an antiseptic pad. "I'll clean that out, OK? It's going to sting."

She whimpers, but I tip her head up. "Hey, no worries. Remember it's not a real hike unless you bruise or bleed."

"Guess this is a real hike then," she grumbles.

The antiseptic does sting, but she grimaces through it, and after about ten minutes, she stands, wobbles a little, and says, "Let's go."

We gain the ridge, hang a left toward North Percy and fight our way past treeline. The girl hits the ledges like a wild child, her hair knotted, mud and blood caking her knees. But something happens to her above treeline, especially on rock scrambles. She becomes an engine, her little dirty legs fire like pistons as she finds grips and steps.

And North Percy is beautiful. Directly to the south towers the equally sharp summit cone of South Percy. As we break onto the wide, flat summit, we can see the rolling slope of yesterday's hike, Sugarloaf, just up the Nash Stream Road.

Janelle just rolls on until we reach the top, stops at the summit sign and puts her leg up on summit cairn. "There!"

We share a high five and I just shake my head. "Way to fight through it," I say.

Heading down off North Percy Peak on a perfect day.

The day is perfect. We explore the enormous summit area and Janelle skips through alpine wild flower groves, the trials of getting up here all but forgotten. I brought a special treat for her on this hike, packaged noodles, which we boil on a portable stove. She lays out our lunch like a picnic and we feast. We celebrate this startling, green and purple summit. We celebrate four days in a row of hiking. We celebrate bruises and blood and mud. We bang our plastic cups of steaming noodles together in a toast to how far we've come and how far we've yet to go, and the day drifts by like a cloud on the horizon.

North Percy Peak

September 3, 2012

SUMMIT ELEVATION 3,430 feet

LOCATION AND DIRECTIONS From Route 3 in Groveton, take Route 110 East 2.6 mi. to Emerson Road (on the left). Follow Emerson Road for 2.2 mi. and turn onto Nash Stream Road. Trailhead parking is reached in 2.7 mi., while the actual trail begins 50 yards further up the road after the bridge over Slide Brook.

OUR ROUTE Percy Peaks Trail to the col between North and South Percy, then left on (unsigned but obvious) North Percy Spur.

TRIP MILEAGE 4.4 miles round trip.

IF YOU GO Nash Stream Road is wide, clear and navigable for any car, but the road is closed to motor vehicle traffic in winter and is primarily used as a snowmobile route.

| 22 |

Of Fungus, Mushrooms, and Algae

#23: Mount Tremont

The girl is in high form, bouncing up the trail like a pinball defying gravity. Perhaps she's getting stronger. Perhaps the trail is moderate and the distance short.

Most likely, she's just a ham around others. Our friends Peter (Alvin the Swede) and Elizabeth (Inchworm) have joined us again for a wet and wild hike up Mount Tremont, an obscure little summit south of Crawford Notch near the Sawyer Ponds.

Today, Tough Cookie is engaged and funny. She's thrilled to be back on the trail after a couple days off. She's even happier that the weather is not quite behaving.

Rain has threatened us all day and a deep moisture permeates the forest as we make our way up the mountain. We expect the skies to open at any moment.

But in the meantime, the dampness has opened up the forest. Mushrooms appear to sprout before our very eyes, deep reds and purples and brilliant whites. Fungus clings to the sides of rotting trees, the morning dew sparkling off the edges like shimmering crystals.

We move more slowly than we normally would as our friends build their hiking legs, but that's perfect for Janelle. She crouches down low at every enormous mushroom or deep purple fungus, in her element.

In quieter moments now, as she tilts her head to peer under a branch at bright orange algae, or lets the wind tear through her already wild hair, I can see shadows of the outdoors woman she might become, perhaps a mountain hut croo member, an environmentalist, a thru-hiker? Those moments are still fleeting as she's young and I'm unclear what the real impact of these adventures will be.

Perhaps her good mood is just that of a hiker, still a child, enjoying the company of friends, being the center of attention, showing us that she knows the names of clouds or can identify a mushroom or two.

Either way, time goes by as it always does in the mountains and together we all laugh and slip in the mud and tell stories, and rain holds and the day rolls on.

Mount Tremont was not always an obscure peak. The long-lost logging town of Livermore existed in the shadow of the mountain to the north. And in the early 1960s, a grand resort called the Sawyer River Skiway was proposed to drop down off nearby Mount Saunders and extend across the Livermore Valley onto the lower slopes of Tremont.

It never happened, and now this area of the lower Crawford Notch is bare, the forest having reclaimed most of Livermore and all but one or two trails in the surrounding area. That makes the small, bare summit of Mount Tremont that much sweeter as the four of us hit the top and spread out along the thin summit rock to take in views of Sawyer Pond and the surrounding scenic area. Even through a low cloudy mist, Green's Cliff is a prominent landmark from our perch.

Someone has painted a smiley face on the USGS marker at the summit. Peter snaps some shots of Janelle and me, and it feels good to be able to play with the kid without worrying about capturing any of my own shots.

Shortly after our arrival, an older hiker arrives and wastes no time inserting himself into our group. He carries an ancient rucksack, and a long knife in a worn scabbard hangs from his hip.

"Hello! Hello!" he says. "Great to see others up here. I figured I'd be alone on a day like this." He sits on the rock right next to Janelle and says, "How are you, young lady?"

I pull an apple out of my pack and make a big show of my own knife as I cut it into pieces. But my worries, as usual, are unfounded. He's all over the place, just happy to see folks. He jumps down to show Peter

Sun-dappled woods
highlight a humid hike
on Mount Tremont.

some other USGS triangulation markers, then spends a long time pointing out other mountains and trails for us.

Like Janelle, he's a big fan of pistachios, and he chats with her at length about the pluses and negatives of red versus green pistachios. He's a comfortable sort, perhaps not fully socialized, or maybe just happy, as most hikers are.

So I let him talk, and soon some distant thunder echoes through the valley, a signal for us to leave. On the way out, it does rain, but for some reason Janelle and I are looking for more. As our friends head home and the drizzle turns to a downpour, we pull up our hoods and pick our way down an embankment near the parking area and walk to the bank of the Saco River.

There, we watch the rushing water in the rain, with drops dripping from our eyelashes, not caring about the thunder, talking of mushrooms and fungus, unwilling to let the day end.

Mt. Tremont

September 8, 2012

SUMMIT ELEVATION 3,371 feet

LOCATION AND DIRECTIONS Harts Location (between Bartlett village and Crawford Notch State Park). The trail begins on the south side of Route 302, 0.5 mi. west of the Sawyer Rock picnic area and a short distance east of the bridge over Stony Brook.

OUR ROUTE Mount Tremont Trail up and back.

TRIP MILEAGE 5.6 miles round trip.

IF YOU GO The parking area for the Mt. Tremont Trail is on the west side of Route 302, about 100 yards north of the trailhead.

| 23 |

Go Ask Alice

#24: Mount Cube

"Dan and Janelle!" Someone is shouting our names.

Two hikers emerge onto the summit of Mount Cube, where we are having lunch. One of them clearly knows us. There is always something a bit disconcerting about being recognized by someone you don't know, but years in journalism and writing have made me somewhat familiar with the experience. But this is the first time such a thing happens to Janelle. I'm curious how she'll react.

Patti is a longtime follower of *The Nepal Chronicles*, my travel blog about my trip with Meena to Nepal, and followed us to *The Adventures* from there. Patti recognizes us through photos on our site. And soon, she is no longer a stranger. Patti is working on her 52WAV list as well. Years ago, she hiked all the 4,000-footers with her son.

Janelle is quiet at first, but begins to open up after a while. She's not a girl who makes friends quickly, the consequence perhaps of years of geographic uncertainly, of being moved around a lot, of not knowing how long any current situation will last. I stay close to her, gauging her reactions and level of comfort, but she seems fine.

After some time spent on Cube's summit, we bid our new friends goodbye and meander over to the mountain's magnificent north ledges which look out over the giant bulk of Mount Moosilauke and Blueberry Mountain. The day is warm and bright and neither of us says anything for a while.

The north-facing ledges of Mount Cube offer Tough Cookie unparalleled views of Mount Moosilauke.

Then, she chirps, "Well, that was weird."

My heart sinks a little, but she notices my distress and quickly adds, "But good weird! Really good! They seem like really nice people."

"You're not just saying that?" I ask.

She shakes her head, smiles and hands me a brownie.

Today has been a day of creatures. Earlier, as we drove down a dusty, dirt road searching for the trailhead, a muddy yellow hound came bounding out of the woods. I slammed on the brakes and the dog happily went on its way, clueless as to its tenuous grasp on this mortal coil.

And just when we were about to hit the trail, a kind woman walking two well-behaved dogs stopped to chat and Janelle had the chance to toss a tennis ball for the larger of the two.

We both love to see dogs on the trail, but Janelle is a little thing and the occasions when a poorly trained pup is near can be stressful. I know parent hikers who carry everything from sprays to clubs, not for fighting off bears but for keeping errant dogs away from their kids.

But we also come across several enormous glistening mushroom fields this day.

"How about that one?" Janelle says, pointing to a giant *Amanita muscaria*, a common toadstool otherwise known as the fly killer.

"Oh, no!" I say. "That's a very poisonous one! Gives you delusions and hallucinations."

"It's pretty," she says wistfully,

"Don't eat it, Alice," I say.

"Who?"

Actually, it's unlikely Lewis Carroll had the fly killer in mind when Alice ate the mushroom in Wonderland. But the *Amanita* does have an interesting history, and it can be eaten if parboiled properly. The mushroom's nickname is thought to come not from its ability to kill flies, but rather from the delirium that comes from eating it and the medieval belief that flies could enter a person's head and cause mental illness. Nice.

We wind back down to the road, Mount Cube behind us, and chat idly about our next hike, our halfway point.

With school in session, our hikes are now limited to weekends and days off, and I worry that the kid is going to get sick and tired of this and just want to play in the alley with her friends.

"How are you doing with this?" I ask.

She tilts her head at me in a way I've come to understand means something like *more details please.*

"Hiking every weekend, you having fun still?"

"Of course!"

She thinks I'm daft, but I push on. "We're going to be spending a lot of time up here in the next few months if we want to finish on schedule," I say. "If we want to get it done before snow."

She does stop and looks at me. "Why would we not hike in snow?"

I honestly have no answer for that.

Mt. Cube   *September 11, 2012*

SUMMIT ELEVATION 2,909 feet

LOCATION AND DIRECTIONS Orford. From Route 25A, 8.3 mi. west of Route 25 in Wentworth and 7.1 mi. east of Route 10 in Orford village, turn south onto Baker Road and proceed 0.9 mi. to the trailhead. Parking is available north of the trailhead on the west side of the road.

OUR ROUTE   Mt. Cube Section of the Cross Rivendell Trail, up and back, with a side trip to the north ledges.

TRIP MILEAGE   5.0 miles round trip.

IF YOU GO   Mt. Cube is a moderate and lovely hike, but gravelly Baker Road can be tricky. Our trailhead should be reachable in the winter as there are homes along the road, but high clearance or four-wheel drive might be needed.

| 24 |

Pushing Our Limits

#25 & #26: Jennings Peak and Sandwich Dome

"We should bring a sandwich," Janelle says as we gear up in the parking lot and prepare for the longest hike of our journey thus far.

I'm distracted, focusing on making sure we have everything we need. "Um-hmm, we have bagels today."

She sighs. "No, because of where we're hiking!"

I finally get her joke. "Right! Sorry."

"Then we could eat a sandwich on Sandwich," she says, infinitely pleased with herself, though this joke has been in her head all week. A mountain named Sandwich has fascinated her to no end.

At 3,980 feet, Sandwich Dome is the tallest on our list and I originally felt it would come later in our quest. But a weather washout the day before gave us both an extra day of rest and we were eager to make up some ground. Eight miles was a full 1.5 miles longer than anything we'd attempted before, but we had to be here sooner or later, so I figured we'd give it a shot and see just how far the girl had come.

"Why would they name the mountain Sandwich?" Janelle asks as we make our way up toward a cliff area called Noon Peak. "Were sandwiches invented in town?"

"Actually, you're close," I say. "The mountain and the town were named after the guy who invented sandwiches."

"What?" she says. "That's awesome! Who?"

"Uh," I should have prepared for this one. "The Earl of Sandwich, I think. Or he was a duke, some such British thing like that."

Actually, the fourth Earl of Sandwich's name was John Montagu and he was a friend of early New Hampshire governor Benning Wentworth. Thus, the naming.

"Awesome," she says. She can't get over the fact that sandwiches were named after a real person. "Is there a guy named 'Bagel'?"

"Er. . . ."

"Or 'Cookie,' like my name. Who is cookie named after?"

"The cookie monster," I say without missing a beat. I'm proud of this answer.

"Dan! I'm being serious here!"

And so it goes, me feeling woefully unprepared to answer her questions, her blowing through the scenic Sandwich Mountain Trail like it's a sidewalk.

The morning slips by pleasantly and we reach the spur path to Jennings Peak. We bundle up against the wind at the ledgy summit. From there, the trail twists us up the mossy and quiet range, and soon we are higher than we've ever been before.

At the summit of Sandwich Dome we meet our very first Forest Service ranger, a kind and enthusiastic young woman named Dylan. Her job for the day has been checking on the expansion of campsites on the ridge to determine erosion and whether the use is harming the beautiful Sandwich Dome ridge.

She's excited to see a ten-year-old up here, and I'm impressed by her engagement, maintaining a level of enthusiasm while at the same time checking to see how Janelle is feeling, where we're heading and what sort of food we have. "I just finished some awesome lentil soup," she says to Janelle. "What are you eating for lunch?" That sort of thing.

When she learns this is peak number 26 for Janelle, halfway through the list, her eyes get wide. "That's so great, congrats," she says.

I take a picture of her with Janelle and wonder if perhaps my hiking partner is just a younger version of this ranger. Tough Cookie certainly has the interest and mindset for a life in the woods, but really, I

The grand view from Sandwich Dome, our 26th peak on the 52er list. Halfway!

haven't a clue. On an earlier hike, Janelle mentioned that she wanted to be a dentist. That would be fine as well.

Later, on our way back, as we're resting near the intersection of the Sandwich Mountain and Drakes Brook trails, a group of hikers comes up from the Drakes Brook Trail and ask for directions to Jennings Peak. We chat and they mention that Drakes Brook passes some waterfalls.

"Can we go down and see that?" Janelle asks.

The new trail would loop us back to the car but would also add a half mile to an already long day.

"I don't care," she says. "I feel fine."

She seems strong and we have no hike tomorrow. So we take the long way home, and at the lower stretch of the trail Janelle sits near a series of waterfalls by Drake's Brook and we finish our tea. She finds a beat path and I let her scramble down to the edge of a crystal pool, where she dips her hand in the water and splashes her face. Then she just sits there for a bit, looking out, watching the waterfalls. I slip down beside her and we finish the day like that, our feet sore, halfway done.

Jennings Peak and Sandwich Dome   *September 15, 2012*

SUMMIT ELEVATIONS Jennings Peak, 3,460 feet; Sandwich Dome, 3,980 feet
LOCATION AND DIRECTIONS Waterville Valley. On Route 49 as you near

Waterville Valley, the trailhead is found on the right side of the highway, 0.4 mi. southwest of the junction with Tripoli Road.

OUR ROUTE Sandwich Mountain Trail, with side trip on Jennings Peak Spur, return trip down Drakes Brook Trail.

TRIP MILEAGE 8.5 miles round trip.

IF YOU GO Sandwich Dome can be reached from several different directions via many routes. Consult the *AMC White Mountain Guide* for the various options.

| 25 |

Be One With the Wet

Our West Royce hike is a muddy, foggy, festering slog over wet rocks covered with moss.

We are in Evans Notch, as close to Maine as we can get, in a section of the White Mountains rarely traveled. The parking lots are empty. The Burnt Mill Brook trail is overgrown and shimmers with morning dew and pervasive moisture. We are wet moments after we set foot on the trail.

But five mountains on our list sit out here, about as far northeast in the Whites as you can go, and we need to start exploring them before the weather turns and roads start closing. In this case, our trail is off the Wild River Road and we have to drive into Maine, then back into New Hampshire to get to it. One can see why the Wild River is called that out here, as it snakes and roars near this backwoods lane, sometimes quite close to the road. In a storm, this river must breech this road easily.

Still, on a cold, wet day like today, West Royce, with its moderate ascent and short distance, seems a perfect fit.

But moderate becomes rough and difficult in weather like this. The trail zigzags harshly up the north side of West Royce Mountain and we struggle against the blowing mist closing over us like a cold blanket.

A stiff wind tears through the trees over our heads and freezing water rains down off the leaves onto us. We are sweating and freezing,

Looking for the summit on the ridge to West Royce Mountain.

chilled and overheated. West Royce is supposed to be a beautiful mountain with far-reaching views. Today, we see nothing. The mountain is angry.

We play guessing games to pass the time, thinking of hiking-related words and giving each other twenty questions to figure them out.

Janelle is in the lead and I watch her silently work her way around slick boulders. She picks a root instead of flat ground, and before I can reach out, she's down in the moss with a thump.

"Argh!" she grumbles. "Stupid roots!" She brushes the dirt and mud off the knees of her pants, jams her poles into the dirt and lifts herself up.

"Blood? Breaks?" I ask.

"No," she says. "Some days are just not good for hiking."

But she does not ask to turn around. She shakes the frigid water out of her hair, takes a deep breath, and moves on.

Indeed, today is not a good day for hiking. But where a day like this used to elicit frustration or even tears, now Janelle screws down that negative emotion and calibrates it into determination. We are here, the summit awaits; weather be damned.

After what seems like a long while, we come to a junction with the Basin Rim Trail, turn right and begin the final ascent to West Royce.

Here, as we work hard the last few tenths of a mile to attain this wet and wild summit, Janelle reveals that she's been working on writing a screenplay for a zombie movie.

"What?" I ask. "You've — What?"

"A zombie movie," she repeats. "Called *Zombies from Black Lake*. Or *Rise of the Zombies*. I haven't figured that out yet, but it will star my friends, and you and Meena can be in it and we'll film it at your cabin — that's where I got the idea for the lake."

I don't know what to say, so she continues, thinking out loud.

"Actually, I don't think I can write it and act in it and direct it, so you'll be the director."

"OK," I say. "Can there be an old man in the film who initially warns the kids of the zombies but they think he's crazy? I can play him."

She thinks about this for a long time as we swing around a ridge and move over ledges that in good weather would provide long and complex views.

"OK, I'll add that," she finally says.

We move up and down the trail near the signed intersection the *AMC White Mountain Guide* says is the summit, but the fog is too thick to see anything.

I move off trail a bit to find a nice bathroom tree and see the concrete pillars of an old summit fire tower, which operated here from 1940 to 1948. The White Mountain guidebook says nothing about this. Janelle and I break through some thick brush and pop out on what I imagine is the true summit, and suddenly the hike takes on meaning.

Even with the four concrete pillars and assorted debris from the old tower, the clearing is charming and ghostly. Mist and fog swirl around us as we unpack our lunch and spread out on what used to be directly under the tower cab.

"This is spooky!" Janelle says, but with a grin.

The fire tower was disassembled in the late 1940s and is now surrounded by a wall of trees and brush, making it secluded and quiet.

We snack there amid the ghosts of tower past and the wind blows above us there on a secluded mountain with no views.

And a raw hike that started with a chill becomes warm and comfortable in the fine remains of that tower. And the girl and I sit and eat peanuts and talk of zombies.

West Royce Mtn. *September 22, 2012*

SUMMIT ELEVATION 3,210 feet

LOCATION AND DIRECTIONS Beans Purchase (near North Chatham). Trailhead is located on Wild River Road, 2.7 mi. south of its intersection with Maine Route 113 in Hastings.

OUR ROUTE Burnt Mill Brook Trail to Basin Rim Trail.

TRIP MILEAGE 5.4 miles round trip.

IF YOU GO The site of the old fire tower is about 30 yards south of the signed intersection. A lightly beaten path to the tower is found on the west side of the trail.

| 26 |

The Challenge Isn't Always the Mountain

#28: Mount Hayes

The pain is blinding.

For a terrifying moment, my vision goes white and I have enough presence of mind to realize that I might pass out. Time really does slow down in a crisis and a wave of thoughts floods into my mind. We are at the summit of Mount Hayes, nearly three miles from the trailhead and another four miles by car from people. Will the girl be able to get off the mountain on her own? Did I teach her well enough? Will I hit my head when I go down?

And finally, how embarrassing will it be to have injured myself by biting into an Oreo cookie? I've cracked a tooth, and as the edge of the broken piece jams into the nerve, a world of hurt roars through my head.

But as quickly as it comes, the pain leaves.

"Are you OK?" Janelle asks. I must have gasped.

"Yup, all good," I say. I touch the broken tooth with my tongue and it causes pain. Ugh.

Janelle and I have a little ceremony at the beginning of each hike where I make her memorize the name of the mountain, the trails we're taking and the town we're in. If she needs to use my cell phone, she needs to know what to tell rescuers. But if there's no signal? If she has to take action instead of waiting for help, what then?

In the course of our journey, we've talked often about finding shelter, staying warm and first aid. She asks questions often, but in a real emergency, will she respond?

We leave the summit area of Hayes and slowly pick our way down to the real reason for climbing this mountain, the magnificent lookouts of the south ledges. From here, the views extend deeply into Pinkham Notch and west down Route 2 and the Northern Presidentials. From here we are not much higher than 2,000 feet, but the views of Gorham and the bigger mountains are unrivaled.

We sit and soak in the sun.

"So kid-o," I begin slowly, "what would you do if I hurt myself and couldn't speak?"

"Call for help."

"What if you couldn't get a signal on the phone and had to rescue us yourself?"

She thinks about this for a long time.

"Well, I'd have to make sure we're warm and safe."

That's about as good as it's going to get. So, there on those ledges, as we sip juice and watch the clouds move over the Carter Range, I begin a more detailed lesson on worst-case scenarios: how a ten-year-old girl could save a grown man, build shelter, provide detailed first aid, start a fire and finally, leave me if she has to rescue herself.

She listens, alert and interested, but she stops me at the part about leaving me.

"I thought you said that the team always sticks together, that we shouldn't ever split up."

"Yes, but we are talking about the worst emergency situations here. If you can't save me, you have — "

"I won't leave you," she interrupts. "You wouldn't leave me, would you?"

"No. Never."

"OK, so I won't leave you."

This ledge on Mount Hayes offers a bird's-eye view of Gorham village and more distant Pinkham Notch.

She's getting emotional, so it's time to move on. But before we can, I notice movement out of the corner of my eye.

"Janelle," I say, "you are going to see something in a second, coming toward you over your pack. Don't freak out."

Of course, she freaks out. "Holy cow, ack! Get it away! Kill it!"

Through rain and wind and long, hard miles, nature has tested Janelle and she has passed. She's held newts and studied slugs and heard the terrifying flapping of nearby grouse, and those encounters have only made her more interested.

But not this.

The half-dollar-sized wolf spider plodding across her pack is too much. The spider's hairy legs bristle in the wind. The spider is so big I can see its eyes. And it does not seem to care one whit about the two humans shrieking at the top of their lungs; Janelle yelling for me to kill it, me trying to calm her down and get a picture of the thing because it's moving so fast.

The spider really is big, the largest I have seen in the Northeast. Wolf spiders do have a bite, but they aren't dangerous. This one, though, looks like a mini-tarantula.

Finally, after we both calm down, Janelle finds a stick and I'm able to lift the thing off her pack and put it on the ground so we can get a good look.

"There, see, we don't have to kill it," I say, only partly believing myself that the spider isn't going to leap up and attack at any moment.

So we get down on the rock and watch the creature power its way over the ledge, seeming to know exactly where to go. When a particularly strong breeze hits the spider, it bunches up its legs, making itself harder to knock over.

Janelle is curious, but this is no toad. After a while, she's had enough and drifts away, calm enough to know that *this* wolf spider won't do her any harm, but not so certain that another one, lurking somewhere, won't be the one that does her in.

Mt. Hayes   *September 23, 2012*

SUMMARY ELEVATION 2,555 feet

SUMMIT ELEVATION 2,555 feet

LOCATION AND DIRECTIONS Gorham. The trail begins on Hogan Road, 0.1 mi. north of a powerhouse and dam on a canal next to the Androscoggin River. To access Hogan Road, follow North Road north from US Route 2 in Shelburne and turn left onto Hogan Road in 0.5 mi. From here's it's a rough and tumble 4.5 mi. to the trailhead.

OUR ROUTE The Mahoosuc Trail, up and back.

TRIP MILEAGE 5.4 miles round trip.

IF YOU GO A hiker used to be able to get to the Mahoosuc Trail off Hogan Road from Route 16 by crossing over a railroad bridge and dam near the trailhead. That route is now closed and one has to drive 4.5 miles along Hogan Road. Do not attempt this road without high clearance as there are several washed out ditches along the way that even our Subaru Forester had trouble negotiating. During mud season this road would be impassable, and the road is unmaintained during the winter.

| 27 |

Everything

#29: Black Mountain (Jackson)

We take our time today. A low mist hangs over Black Mountain, cool but not cold. It won't rain on this hike, but the air is thick and drowsy. We begin in our rain gear, but peel it off and decide to just hike through the warm damp. The quiet forest speaks volumes today and we slowly make our way up a wide overgrown ski trail; the girl and I say little.

The Black Mountain Trail provides a short hike to the cabin at the top of Jackson, but we have no expectations of views so are free to be slow, to hike without expectations, to simply be with each other as there is nothing else to engage us. Or so I think.

About halfway up the mountain, we come to a split in the trail, like a green meridian, a small forest in the middle of the trail. Janelle walks right into it. "Can we take a break here?"

"Sure."

I sit on a rock next to her and watch her dig around in the soil.

Then, she holds her hand out to me. On her pinky rests a tiny, pinhead-sized, speck of leaf.

"What's that?" I ask.

"That's the hiker," she says. "Watch."

She bends over and places the speck-hiker under a six-inch spruce seedling in the middle of the trail.

"I sometimes like to think that there's a tiny forest," she says. "The hiker is walking through it like we are."

The little spruce becomes an enormous tree, a pebble becomes a giant boulder. Twigs and grass and other flecks are all part of the mini-forest landscape.

"A forest inside a forest," I say, and she nods happily. I watch her play inside her tiny forest for a while, considering the depth of this innocent display.

Hiking with Janelle has turned me inward, at first *forced* me to look more closely at the miniature of the forest. But in time, that closer examination has become expansive, comfortable and infinite. A forest inside a forest. Endless forests within the greater landscape, the natural world expanding exponentially even as our place in it becomes smaller. We are hiking on a micro-level, just as we live as tiny specks within the greater universe, dust motes, blinks of an eye.

How present of her then. How engaged. Her inadvertent Buddhist moment of waking life is a child's normal state of being; a fleeting second away from her troubles, of the past and of the future. We are together in nature of our own making, now, fully alive.

We are free, here, in this forest, our forest, together in the face of the endless and impossible everything.

"See?" she asks and there is no end to the depth and expanse of her question.

I do.

Black Mountain   *September 24, 2012*

SUMMIT ELEVATION 2,757 feet

LOCATION AND DIRECTIONS Jackson. From Wentworth Hall in Jackson, follow Carter Notch Road 3.7 mi. to Melloon Road. Turn onto Melloon Road and the trailhead is reached in another 0.3 mi.

OUR ROUTE Black Mountain Ski Trail, up and back.

TRIP MILEAGE 3.4 miles, round trip.

IF YOU GO The Black Mountain cabin is available to rent for overnight stays through the Saco District Ranger Station (603–447–5448) in Conway.

| 28 |

Use It Until You Break It, and Then Use It Some More

> #30: North Doublehead

We hear the giggling first.

Then they appear, two girls from out of the mist and rain. They are wet, muddy and happy. The older one, about Janelle's age, is being pulled by a huge, gray dog, large enough that she could ride it up and down the mountain. The smaller girl, perhaps 7, wears a bright green and yellow rain slicker with turtle patterns. She leads a tiny dog, so wet and dripping that its fur drags in the mud.

Rain is falling and thick clouds hang low in the valley. Janelle and I were just about to begin the long slog to the summit of North Double-head when the two girls appeared, coming down from the trail, and bee-lined to a car parked next to ours. "Hi!" they both say at once. The older one reaches into her raincoat and pulls out car keys and opens the door of the van next to us.

We look on, wondering if the ten-year-old is going to drive away. Boy, they start them early in the North Country!

"Beat your parents down, huh?" I say.

"Uh-hmm." The older one laughs. "Good thing we got her keys!"

I glance over at Janelle, but she's just watching them: two kids, her age, tackling the rain and cold and not seeming to care. She's badly wanted to hike with someone her age, but such kids have not been

North Doublehead Mountain offers a cabin nearly identical to its twin on Black Mountain.

easy for us to find. I wish she'd just come out and talk to them, make friends, ask them to hike with us next time.

"Did you have a nice hike?" I ask them.

"Great!" The little one is shaking with energy, or trying to stay warm. It's hard to tell. "You hike up into a cloud."

We need their enthusiasm, feed off it. Five minutes ago, this hike was going to be a mud march. Now, Janelle is smiling.

"Ready to hike up into a cloud?" I ask her.

She grins. "Number 30," she says. "Let's go!"

The rain comes, then goes, then comes back. It drizzles, then pours, then stops entirely, then a low misty fog hangs thickly over the mountain. We climb up the wide ski trail. Mushrooms, emboldened by the damp, burst forth from dead tree trunks, and glowing yellow and orange fungus greets us around every turn.

The ski trail continues to the left, but we make a sharp right halfway up and this new trail switchbacks up into the col between North and South Doublehead.

There's one steep pull before the ridge, and as we turn right and head straight up the slope, Janelle slips on a wet root and jams her pole into the soft earth to recover. In so doing, her hiking pole bends cleanly into a sharp right angle.

"No!" she says. "Oh, no!"

She received the poles as a gift from her grandmother whom the kids affectionately call Nana Banana, and has used them regularly. They are blood red, and now scarred from miles of use. They have meaning to her.

But they are not expensive and easily replaced.

"I can't believe this," she says. "I didn't do anything, it just broke. Now what?"

She's spinning into panic, or a tantrum. Is it guilt, perhaps, over breaking gear? An automatic child's response to not wanting to get into trouble?

"Hey, hey, it's okay," I say. "Stuff breaks out here all the time. Just means you're using it, which is all your grandma would want to hear, right?"

She's not crying, but tears could come. I slip off my pack and we sit down in the trail.

"Really, no one is going to be mad at you," I say. "And Christmas is only a couple months away. We have extra poles at home, we'll just mix and match for now."

"What do we do today?"

"Nothing. Use the pole until the thing snaps in half. Then we'll go home, put it into our hiking hall of fame and replace the sucker with another one you can break."

"Okay," she says glumly, but she's grinning. Crisis averted. I want her to understand the difference between misuse and overuse. No hiker wants broken gear, but if it breaks because of constant and proper use, well, there's nothing wrong with that.

After a few more twists and turns, we break out into a clearing and the North Doublehead cabin comes into view. Built and maintained as a self-service lodge for backcountry skiers, the cabin sleeps about eight. And like the cabin atop Black Mountain yesterday, Janelle is instantly and entirely entranced by the idea of sleeping there overnight. She begins adding up friends and family who could make this hike with us so we can fill the place with eight people. And I must admit for about $30 a night, it's a good deal.

The cabin is locked now, so we kick around the summit a bit, checking out the brand new and huge outhouse and searching for views. But thick clouds hang deeply into the valley and we see nothing.

We eat lunch, and the rain changes from a drizzle to a downpour, but we hold on as long as we can up there, enjoying the day. Finally, the rain is too much, and as the skies open up we grab our gear, bent and broken and dirty, and hustle off the summit, the torrent at our backs.

North Doublehead   *September 25, 2012*

SUMMIT ELEVATION 3,053 feet

LOCATION AND DIRECTIONS Jackson. From Route 16A in Jackson village, turn onto 16B at the Jackson Post Office. Continue 2.2 mi. to Black Mountain Ski Area, where you turn right, and then right again in another 0.2 mi. onto Dundee Road. The trailhead is reached in another 0.5 mi., or 2.9 mi. total from Jackson village.

OUR ROUTE Doublehead Ski Trail to Old Path to summit, up and back.

TRIP MILEAGE 3.0 miles round trip.

IF YOU GO Like Black Mountain, the Doublehead cabin is available to rent for overnight stays through the Saco Ranger District Station (603–447–5448) in Conway. Warning: Dundee Road is not maintained in the winter.

| 29 |

New Lessons

> #31: Imp Face

"What a brave little girl," the man says, "climbing such big mountains!"

We are near the Imp Face ledge. The trail is wet. There's a storm coming. Tomorrow morning, along with Meena, we'll set off into the wilderness toward Stairs Mountain for an overnight backpack. It will be the first time Janelle will experience a night in the backcountry, so we're eager to get back to camp to prepare for that. But we don't want to let a free day go by without tagging a peak.

Imp Face, a craggy ledge of Middle Carter Mountain that juts out into Pinkham Notch, is a good way to warm up for the trials of the coming days and quickly tick off one of the short hikes left on our list.

But we're hiking during a holiday weekend, in prime leaf-peeper season, so the roads and trails are saturated with tourists. These two caught up with us, but they're sucking wind pretty badly and appear to have only one plastic water bottle between them.

"Sooooo brave!" he says again in a heavy German accent. His companion nods vigorously in agreement.

I don't know if he's being condescending, or perhaps there is something lost in the translation. Maybe he's complimenting her, but it comes out sounding like surprise instead of praise. Though perhaps surprise *is* praise. But I really don't know. We have had no experience

A burst of color makes for an enjoyable fall foliage hike to the Imp Face.

yet with doubters, though from friends who hike big mountains with kids, I know they are out there.

Janelle looks up at me. I want to tell the guy that he has no idea how brave she is, how this is mountain number 31 for her, how we've hiked in ice and rain, and how Janelle has dedicated all her free time to this pursuit out of passion and determination. I want to tell him that this is not about being brave anyway. Her being up here is about being prepared and smart. I want to say that literally anything is possible.

Instead, I take the lazy path. "She sure is!" I say.

Later, I feel like I've betrayed Janelle, like she had looked to me for something more, for a greater defense of her accomplishments.

"Listen, about that guy," I begin, "I should have said more. I'm sorry."

She's puzzled. "Why?" She shrugs. "He had a crazy accent, I couldn't understand a word he said."

I'm glad to have been able to dodge a potential negative moment, but little did we both know what was ahead.

But for today, autumn is in full, glorious bloom and the forest is bathed in an orange, red and yellow glow. The trail to Imp Face is not difficult, though the leaf-covered ground makes footing tricky.

The trail comes right to the edge of a ravine that overlooks Town-line Brook, hangs a sharp right and zigzags up a little rocky rise before finally popping out on the Imp Face ledges.

This ledge was given its name because supposedly, from near Dolly Copp Campground, it appears as a distorted human face. I've never been able to see a resemblance, but White Mountain lore is replete with such colorful names. At any rate, Imp Face is a beautiful ledge, offering visitors wide uninterrupted views south down Pinkham Notch and west to the Presidentials.

Unfortunately, at nearly the moment we step out onto the ledge, it begins to drizzle. There's a bigger set of storm clouds coming up from the valley and we can see the deep gray rainclouds moving toward us from the south.

"We don't have much time," I say. "Gear up."

She hesitates. Even after thirty mountains, Janelle is still learning to function in inclement weather on her own. She still needs to be gently nudged when it comes to concepts of layering, and she does not like taking off and putting back on, based on conditions.

"Rain jacket, hat, get your gloves ready," I say.

"Do we have time to eat?" she asks, eying the oncoming storm warily.

"Sure, gear first. Then, we eat lunch."

We move off the ledges and under the cover of some thick pines and get our rain gear ready. A sharp wind picks up and slides over the ledges and we turn our backs to the views and hunker down to eat. Our lunch is cut short by the not-so-distant rumble of thunder.

"Oh-oh!" Janelle says. And soon we're hustling off the summit, down back through the ravine, and we make it all the way to a long straightaway through a grand strand of hemlocks before the skies really open up on us.

As echoes of thunder ring through the valley and the rain polishes the colored leaves to an intense, glossy glow, I stop the girl and our hurried descent. We're under the canopy cover. We're safe. There's no reason to not enjoy the fall.

I pull her close and snap an arm's-length photo of us there in the bright forest, rain on our glasses, smiles on our faces. Ready for tomorrow.

Imp Face

SUMMIT ELEVATION 3,165 feet

LOCATION AND DIRECTIONS Martins Location (south of Gorham). The trailhead for the north branch of the Imp Trail is located on Route 16 about 2.6 mi. north of the Mt. Washington Auto Road entrance and 5.4 mi. south of Gorham village.

OUR ROUTE Imp Trail, north branch.

TRIP MILEAGE 4.4 miles round trip.

IF YOU GO We took the Imp Tail up to Imp Face and back, but the trail can also be used as a loop that ends back at Route 16 a short distance from where you begin.

| 30 |

Remember Friends

#32 & 33: Mount Crawford and Stairs Mountain

Hours ago, at the trailhead, I put my backpack on the willing shoulders of Janelle, and the crazy child sauntered around the parking lot with forty pounds on her back, grinning foolishly, the adrenaline of the coming hike giving her strength and energy.

Now, as we make our way up to the open summit of Mount Crawford, the weight of that pack pushing pleasantly on my shoulders, I watch Janelle and Meena pick their way through the ledges and, despite the ache in my knees, I think *This is where I want to be.*

Atop Crawford, we sit in the open, the Dry River Wilderness at our feet, considering distant Stairs Mountain, sometimes called The Giant Stairs, so named because that's what it looks like. Our goal is to spend the night tonight at the top of those stairs. We have darkness, and a coming snowstorm, to beat.

At the summit of Crawford, someone has erected a cairn of brightly colored stones. Atop the pile is a small stone-carved bird. Two stones have words on them: "Remember Friends."

I look back on that moment now with sorrow. As the three of us sat atop that beautiful peak, the colors of autumn sparkling around us, together and happy, a friend I called my sister was losing her years-long battle with cancer. We would not hear this news until the next evening.

After Crawford, we move deep into the wilderness, down through

The wilderness spreads out before Short Step and Tough Cookie as they make their way off Mount Crawford.

a beautiful rocky open area, and hike right up to the base of Resolution Mountain. There we make a left, and the trail spins us around the base toward Stairs. Tomorrow, we'll hike up Resolution on our way out of the wilderness. We've parked Meena's car on the opposite side so we won't have to double back.

But today, as we hike up the side of Stairs to the campsite at the top, we are tired. Darkness is dropping and a deep, unsettling quiet has settled over the summit of Stairs Mountain. Tonight is Janelle's first time in the woods after dark, away from the security of cars, camp stores and washrooms. Exposed. Snow is coming.

Janelle is engaged, eager. She helps set up camp. She carried the tent poles up here, so she might as well be the one to assemble them. Her job is to unpack and sort our food, which she does with enthusiasm and efficiency. We have a hot dinner of rice and noodles and sit on the magnificent ledges of Stairs' summit until the granite chills and the sun can no longer provide any hope of warmth.

Now, Janelle begins to shiver a little and she starts to worry, the ache in her bones from the day's hike combined with this new experience taking its toll. Meena takes her to the tent, layers her up and tucks her in her bag to show her how warm she'll be, snow or no snow.

I give my survival skills a spin, and mostly fail.

I can't start a fire. I should be able to. I have a lighter and a candle. Yet, even with those tools, I am hopeless. There at the summit of Stairs Mountain, I learn another important lesson. When everything is wet, it's hard to start a fire. Pretty simple.

So I go to Plan B, my Jetboil cooking stove. I spend ten minutes boiling water on the stove, which we'll put back in our water bottles, then tuck into Janelle's bag: radiators for the night.

There's too much to worry about on a night like this for a ten-year-old who wanted so badly to "camp out in a place where there are no bathrooms," as she said over and over in the past. So I don't want her to have any memory except how beautiful a night on a mountain can be.

We give her attention, and talk to her about our own experiences in camp: coyotes howling us to sleep in the Grand Canyon, camping in the shadow of George Washington's visage at Mount Rushmore, watching the moon rise over Mount Everest in Nepal.

Finally, one last thing before we sleep. We take her out of the tent, into the darkness, out to the ledges. I hold her left hand, Meena holds her right. We stand there at 3,500 feet, three souls breathing hard into the first swirls of snow. I count to three and we all shut off our headlamps.

Our campsite atop Stairs Mountain is only a few feet from the ledges.

Nothing Says "North Country" Like Your First Moose

"Oh my God, stop the car, can we stop the car!" Janelle is freaking out.

This weekend is Labor Day, and the notches are clogged with tourists snapping pictures of leaves. And now this. We round a bend and the state road suddenly becomes a parking lot.

There are easily a dozen cars and perhaps fifty people running this way and that. I've seen this before. A moose.

Sure enough, as we inch our way past the traffic jam, there he is, a young bull, idly munching grass not five feet off the shoulder.

Janelle goes completely bonkers.

As it happens, she is not with me. She's behind me, driving in Meena's car. Janelle's reaction is relayed to me later from Meena. We're on our way to our most difficult hike, an overnighter atop Stairs Mountain. We are already late.

But this is one New Hampshire hiker rite of passage I'm determined Janelle will experience. So, Meena and I pull over, I grab a camera and we become one with the tourists.

In our journey thus far, we have studied moose tracks and discovered more moose scat than we have known what to do with. Once, near the summit of Mt. Roberts, we found a moose bed so fresh that the grass was still unbending as we came across it.

But until now, no actual moose.

Janelle is hesitant as Meena takes her hand and leads her through traffic to the other side of the road. The girl gets about thirty feet from the animal and just stops and watches. There are others getting much, much closer. The animal appears to not care, but I've seen enough "Animals Go Wild" Discovery Channel specials to know what will happen if some unthinking tourist blocks off the moose's retreat route. So, we keep our distance and that's fine.

No hiker earns her true stripes without a moose sighting. This one posed for us along Route 302 near Crawford Notch.

"Good timing," Meena quips. "This one ought to be on the New Hampshire Tourism Department payroll."

The idea of paying moose to stand along the side of the road for tourists is a good one. I have visions of acting tryouts, hourly wages and moose actors' guilds.

Janelle creeps up a couple more feet, then turns toward us. A shy grin spreads across her face. We all understand this is an important moment. Yes, this particular moose is on display for all to see. And yes, to some, seeing a moose is a fairly common occurrence.

But to Tough Cookie, this is an earned experience forged in miles hiked and heightened expectations.

And as we march back to our cars to begin our hike, she says. "Do you think we'll see a bear?"

And as we look down across the blackness of the Dry River Wilderness at the distant lights of Jackson, twinkling like stars, I hear Janelle catch her breath. She's never been here before, never looked down on the world from the dark, from above.

"Wow," she whispers into the glorious, cold night.

Mt. Crawford and Stairs Mtn.   *October 7, 2012*

SUMMIT ELEVATIONS Mt. Crawford, 3,119; Stairs Mtn., 3,463 feet

LOCATION AND DIRECTIONS Harts Location. The paved Davis Path parking lot is situated on the north side of Route 302 between Crawford Notch and Bartlett village. The lot is across from the Notchland Inn, 5.6 miles from the Willey House site in Crawford Notch State Park and 6.3 miles from the center of Bartlett at Bear Botch Road.

OUR ROUTE Davis Path (with side trip up Mount Crawford spur) to Stairs Mountain spur.

TRIP MILEAGE 5.2 miles one way, including 0.6 mile up and back to Mt. Crawford.

IF YOU GO A hiker can officially camp atop Stairs Mountain. There are no platforms or amenities, but there are clearly two or three spaces where tents can be pitched. Though only five miles long, this is a strenuous hike and should not be taken lightly. However, the rewards of this little used campsite are great.

| 31 |

Joy and Agony

Janelle wakes up gasping. At first, we think she's had a bad dream or some sort of anxiety attack. But after taking a couple breaths, I realize I'm having a hard time breathing as well.

"I can't sleep," Janelle moans.

It's about midnight. Outside our tent, a wet and steady snow falls. Stairs Mountain is perfectly quiet. If you listen hard enough you can hear the flakes touching down on our tent. Inside, we're warm, but there's something wrong. Meena notices it first.

"Open the vents," she says from the other side of the tent. Janelle is between us.

The vents! I slip out of my bag, feeling lightheaded, and quickly unzip the ceiling vents. Our tent is a heavy winter Nemo, waterproof and designed for the worst above-treeline weather. I also applied sealant to the seams, making the structure indestructible. But apparently, along with being waterproof, the thing is air-proof.

The ceiling has mesh vents for air, overlain by fabric flaps that keep the rain out. I'd forgotten to unzip the fabric flaps before we went to bed. Soon we're all breathing easy, and the rest of the night goes by without incident.

The morning arrives cold but clear as we pick our way down off Stairs, regain the col between the two mountains and head back up toward Resolution.

Looking back at Stairs Mountain from the ledges on Mount Resolution.

Snow on a mountaintop overlooking a beautiful valley is romantic. Frosty, crisp ledges against deep autumn colors are unlike any other hiking experience. But today I'm only thinking about the cold.

We have more than seven miles to hike to our car, over two more mountains. We climb up Resolution at a steady pace, our boots crunching in the frost. When the sun is out, the day warms quickly. When it is not, the cold bites through our fleece. When we move, we are warm. When we pause for pictures or for snacks, we are not.

I'm used to the challenges of this situation. Janelle is not. To her, reaching a summit, or an overlook, is reason to stop, sip tea, perhaps explore a little. But now, our morning consists of movement. The ledges of Resolution are above 3,000 feet and packed with pines and alpine bushes, now hanging low from the night's snow. As we push through the trail, the snow and ice rain down on us and we have to shrug off the cold with every step.

But she is a trooper, still excited from the morning's camp duties and the peanut butter sandwich breakfast we ate while we watched the mist move up and overtake the mountains from below. I watch her, listening for any indication of discomfort. She marches on, carrying more weight than she's ever hauled, her cheeks pink, her fleece hat pulled down till it touches her glasses.

"She's fine," Meena says from over my shoulder.

I kiss my wife, thankful for her company, and we watch together as Janelle pitches forward down the rock, solid, steady. She realizes we've stopped and turns to wait for us. When I catch up, she says, "You lead, Dan."

She wants to be between us, or perhaps more accurately, she wants to be near Meena.

The two have been practicing their whistling skills all weekend and they continue now. And so we hike on, and behind me the cool mountain air is filled with whistles, one sharp and melodic, the other young and barely a whisper. I listen to them whistle, and giggle, and whistle some more, and that calms me and warms me, and my steps become light and the trail no longer seems that long.

Mount Parker is a joy. By the time we reach our fourth summit in two days, we are all beat, but we stand and look back on the big miles we've accomplished and that takes the sting off. The ladies have been teasing me all day about the packet of freeze-dried chicken salad I brought for lunch, but now as we sit on Parker's summit they wolf down the food like it's high-end sirloin. I laugh, and Meena says between bites, "It'd be better on crackers!"

The hike down is gentle and ends with a long logging path straightaway. We have hiked nearly thirteen miles in two days over four mountains. In the snow! We high-five and hug, and as we all climb into Meena's car, I turn on my cell phone and receive the news that my friend has died.

I stay calm, but as we approach my car, I ask Meena to follow me while Janelle waits behind. There, out of sight of the girl, I tell Meena the terrible news. Janelle is close friends to my friends' kids, and I don't know how to break this to her.

"I'll do it," Meena says. "I'll take her and we'll meet you up the road at Fabyans. And I'll order us food. You call them and see how they are."

I'm deeply grateful and am barely able to watch them drive away before sliding down on the bumper of my car and crying, lost in the exhaustion and exhilaration of this weekend's accomplishments and of the renewed understanding of how precious and fleeting this journey truly is.

Mt. Resolution and Mt. Parker   *October 8, 2012*

SUMMIT ELEVATIONS Mt. Resolution, 3,415 feet; Mt. Parker, 3,004 feet

LOCATION AND DIRECTIONS Harts Location and Bartlett. The paved Davis
Path parking lot is situated on the north side of Route 302 between
Crawford Notch and Bartlett village. The lot is across from the
Notchland Inn, 5.6 miles from the Willey House site in Crawford Notch
State Park and 6.3 miles from the center of Bartlett at Bear Botch Road.
The Mt. Landgon Trail, which was our end point, may be reached by
following River Street north across the Saco River from the four-way
intersection in Bartlett village at Bear Notch Road. At a T-intersection
reached in 0.4 mi., turn left and the trailhead and a small parking area
are found a short distance up the road on the right.

OUR ROUTE Our hike began from the top of Stairs Mountain, where we
camped the previous night. We took the Stairs Mountain spur back to
the Davis Path, then headed south on Mt. Parker Trail to Mt. Langdon
Trail.

TRIP MILEAGE 7.2 miles one way.

IF YOU GO Resolution and Parker can be reached individually or together
as a day hike, depending on where you decide to begin. Parker alone is
worth the hike for the views into the Dry River Wilderness.

| 32 |

Rock Stars

#36: Mount Shaw

In New Hampshire family hiking circles, climbing with Trish, Alex and Sage Herr is the big leagues, like tossing baskets with Michael Jordan or having Donald Hall read your poetry. The trails the Herr family has blazed are legendary.

Trish wrote a book about her journey climbing the state's 4,000-foot mountains with her young daughter, Alex. Titled *Up: A Mother and Daughter's Peakbagging Adventure*, the book details their sometimes difficult but always joyful journey. Alex became the second-youngest girl to hike those mountains. A couple years later, her sister Sage bumped Alex down to third on that list.

The three have graciously agreed to hike with us just after getting home from a whirlwind highpointing trip where they bagged three peaks in the Southwest over 13,000 feet.

In the days leading up to our hike up Mount Shaw with the ladies (along with their dad, Hugh), Janelle and I found time to relax at our cabin and Janelle read me passages from Trish's book.

Occasionally, she'd pause at a long word or phrase that confused her.

"This is an adult book," Janelle said at one point. "She uses very big words!"

"I know. But you can read it; you can read to that level."

Despite some difficulty, she did read the book, paying close atten-

Alex and Sage Herr join Janelle atop Mount Shaw.

tion to a chapter on how Alex was faced with an adult who doubted her ability to hike mountains. That chapter and the lessons learned from it would be important to us in a just a few weeks.

But for now, as we pull into the parking area at the base of the mountain, I am tired, strung out and fighting depression. Yesterday was my friend's funeral service and the events of the past week weigh heavily on my mind. The Herr family is already there, happily going about the business of gearing up. I worried all night about how Janelle would handle hiking with Alex and Sage. But apparently, that's just me.

Janelle doesn't have stars in her eyes. She just sees two kids, about her age, who can climb mountains, like her. She sees peers — and girls, no less.

I should have learned this lesson from her time last spring in the fitness program Girls on the Run. Maybe it is as easy as finding other kids who feel the same joy she does and letting them loose on the mountain. Maybe I've been over-thinking this whole thing.

The three met once before, briefly, but not on a trail. The speed and extent of their bonding is nearly alarming. It is as though they have been friends all along. The three little ones barrel up the mountain like tiny locomotives, instant friends.

As usual, at first I worry. Will Janelle be able to keep up? She's soft-spoken and intense. Will Alex and Sage's sisterly bond and outgoing manner be too much for her? Will she be fussy, or have I taught her well enough to hike with far more seasoned hikers?

Will she make me look bad?

Such pedestrian concerns, so adult of me and yet so childish. After a time, my foolish worries evaporate like the morning chill, replaced by wonder. I watch her interact, hike and laugh. The adults are there when the kids trip, or need a break or maybe some trail directions. But today Janelle doesn't actually *need* me, not when Alex and Sage are there with her. Perhaps not when any kids of her age and ability are there with her.

I swallow hard at the thought and quicken my pace just a little, unwilling to let her lose sight of me quite yet.

This small mountain in the Ossipees offers us a nearly perfect fall hike. The trail is not well marked, but it's wide and moderate and before long we find ourselves winding up what appear to be carriage roads to the summit. There, the girls have no use for the fussy adults and find a grassy ledge in the sun to sit and chat and eat their chocolate and granola.

And then it comes to me. As I watch the three of them — tiny things against the enormous backdrop of the White Mountains — I understand how this can happen, what drives Tough Cookie.

To Alex and Sage, being here is not unusual, not a fleeting moment or vacation away from everyday life. This is everyday life.

And as Janelle sits between the two of them, laughing, absorbing their energy, it's clear that she understands that as well. And wants it. And so do I.

Mt. Shaw   *October 13, 2013*

SUMMIT ELEVATION 2,990 feet

LOCATION AND DIRECTIONS Moultonborough. From Route 25 in
   Moultonborough, turn right (southeast) onto Route 109, then left
   onto Route 171 East. The trailhead is unmarked but can be found on
   the right, just after Sodom Road.

OUR ROUTE: Mt. Shaw Trail up and back (with 1.0 mile round trip on the
   spur path to Black Snout Mountain).

TRIP MILEAGE: 8.0 miles round trip.

IF YOU GO   There is some confusion over this trail. The latest edition of the *AMC Southern New Hampshire Guide* (2010), warns of a land dispute near the bottom of this trail and suggests taking another. That dispute must be smoothed over, as the trail is wide, well used and fairly well-marked with dark red blazes. There were half a dozen cars in the parking area and a dozen or so hikers on the trail when we were there. That said, it may be best to use extra caution, stay on the trails, and not overextend your welcome.

Post-Hike Food, and the Lost Art
of the Gas Station Sandwich

There was a time when gas stations were mom and pop businesses, when you'd stop for a fill-up and a sandwich and you weren't playing a game of chicken with ring-worm. Janelle and I spent a lot of time in the car, and a lot of time in the car hungry after a hike.

We tried to stay away from fast food, and didn't have the budget to eat at a restaurant every time. So, one of our goals was to find gas station food that wasn't just eatable, but somewhat healthy and tasty as well.

This was not an easy task, but there are two places we found that made their food fresh each morning, that took pride in their gas station cuisine, and that served as our fallbacks many times.

Along the I-93 corridor, no place comes close to the egg salad sandwiches served at the Kancamagus Country Store in Lincoln. The bread is usually wheat, the sandwiches are made fresh every day and don't suffer from chain store blandness. Plus, we found deviled eggs, ham and cheese, and baloney and mustard to mix things up.

Meanwhile, up north in Gorham, no place does ham salad like Moe's Variety at the junction of Routes 2 and 16. The key to this gas station masterpiece is chopped up pickle bits in the sandwich. Very British!

Another food game we played involved Snapple. Janelle loves Snapple, so we began seeking new flavors. In all, over the course of our quest, we tried about twenty different types. In fact, Janelle kept a journal list. We tried to interest Snapple in sponsoring us, but they were uninterested in two hikers traveling around the state sampling their product. Seemed a perfect fit to us.

By the way, Janelle's favorite flavor was the limited edition Maroon Five Berry Mix.

Along the way, we found other throwbacks to food service at gas stations, from roasted nuts to freshly made pizza to fried chicken so salty and fresh we sat in the car after a late weekday hike and closed our eyes to the world and ate like we never had before.

In many cases, the food tasted so good because of our hunger and weariness. But more often than not, having a secondary quest—finding good cheap food—gave us something to look forward to once we got back to our car.

If you do end up stopping for a bite, tell them Buffalo and Tough Cookie sent you!

| 33 |

Teamwork on Our Longest Hike

> #37, 38, 39 & 40: Eastman Mountain,
> North & South Baldface, and Eagle Crag

Janelle is dragging, not because she is tired or the weather isn't cooperating. In fact, we had plenty of sleep last night, and for mid-October the weather is as clear and warm as possible.

Rather, she knows that her hiking friends Alex and Sage are here, one trail and a couple of miles over, and she badly wants to be hiking with them. The Herr ladies, along with a whole troop of some of our favorite hikers, are taking a different route up toward the Baldfaces; we left earlier and are slogging our way up Eastman Mountain. We'll join them in a couple of hours to complete their's and our's loop. But Eastman is on our list, the mountain is near the Baldfaces, and once we reach the ridge we can just hop over to join the others.

This makes for a long day, more than thirteen miles, the longest day-hike of our journey. But Evans Notch is far off the beaten path, the day is beautiful, and after 30-plus mountains, Janelle is ready.

But first we must tag Eastman.

No amount of cajoling, encouragement or reason seems to be working. Alex and Sage, those two equally tough hiker girls, are within shouting distance and the universe has conspired to put Janelle just out of their reach. I'm not particularly concerned about our inchworm speed, but we did set a time and place on the mountain to meet them

My favorite shot of the joy we feel when hiking, this time atop North Baldface.

and I'm worried only that we're going to be late and they will have to sit at some windy perch getting cold waiting for us.

There's nothing I can do. Alas, the real victim here is Eastman Mountain. The trail is wide and gentle and the forest a swirl of color, making this obscure peak a worthy destination in and of itself. But Eastman will just be a footnote in Janelle's journey, the mountain we *had* to climb in order to get to Alex and Sage. I settle in to our pace, and accept our fate, and the girl and I move up Eastman with thoughts of our friends weighing heavily on our minds.

We reach the summit thirty minutes behind schedule, but take our time at Eastman's bald knob. The view of the Doubleheads to the south and of our destinations, the Baldheads to the north, is clear and beautiful. So clear, in fact, that we share a wordless look that says *we have a long way to go today.*

After a break, we backtrack off the summit, regain the ridge and point our boots toward the Baldfaces. The trail moves gently along the ridge, then shoots straight up a rocky shelf to the top of a minor peak called Bald Knob. We crest that ridge, nearly an hour behind schedule, break out into the open and see our friends, tiny dots, waiting for us at a junction near the bottom of South Baldface.

Tough Cookie powers up a ridge near South Baldface.

Meeting friends in the wilderness is always risky. With no phone signal and changing weather, plans don't always work out. But today, under clear blue skies and milder temps, we all greet each other like long-lost explorers. Janelle is so happy to reunite with Alex and Sage, I can barely keep up with her as we crest the final ridge and join our friends.

Besides Hugh, Trish and the girls, there is Mark and Natalie, a Rhode Island couple who completed their 4,000-footers on the same day Janelle and I battled the wolf spider atop Mount Hayes. On that hike, Natalie fell and opened a wound on her forehead, but that was a final 4,000-footer hike! Undaunted, she completed her journey.

Michael and Donna, trail names Jimmylegs and Little D, round out our team. The Maryland couple are here visiting. This is the first time I have met the two, but I am very familiar with Michael's fine photography and have followed his work closely.

I am thrilled to be a part of this group of all-star hikers. For too long, Janelle and I have explored our mutual path, mostly alone. We've hiked with a friend or two, but this day is different. These hikers are all veterans of the hills, all with stories of their own in pursuit of many other journeys, some complete, some still in progress.

I miss Meenakshi and wish she were with us.

The girls immediately find a glorious ledge and get to building a bench out of flat stones as the adults reacquaint themselves with each other. I'm relieved to hear that the group was also delayed by the more difficult than expected east ledges of South Baldface and arrived only a few minutes before us.

We make quick work of the climb up to South Baldface and pause at the top to eat. Trish breaks out a whole tray of brownies, and we feast there and express wonder that this series of peaks is not more explored. The lure of the 4,000-footer keeps many from this series of summits, and that's a shame. The Baldfaces are as beautiful and challenging as any 4,000-footer, in some cases more so.

The team heads north along the ridge and I listen in as the girls talk about their favorite foods and happiest moments hiking. Janelle mentions that the food she dislikes the most is arugula and I feel a flash of pride knowing that for her to even know what that is, Meena and I must be doing something right.

We all take turns walking in line, each of us sharing our stories because that's what hikers do. In the mountains, it's rare to encounter politics, religion or any of the other meaningless controversies that ball us up in our everyday lives. Here, we are hikers only.

North Baldface comes quickly, and we once again pause for pictures and snacks. I'm struck by Janelle's strength. Looking back, I understand that her energy came from the companionship of friends and the girls were able to feed off each other; no ten-year-old hikes thirteen miles easily, but together, the three forged a team that helped them fight the exhaustion of such a hike.

We drop down off North Baldface with the sun setting at our backs and once again climb up to the ledges of Eagle Crag for our final summit of the day.

Atop the Crag, with the full distance of our hike on display behind us, I take a moment to consider how far we've come on this journey. Being contemplative among the good cheer of our new hiking friends is not easy. But that's a good thing.

Janelle draws faces in sparkling mica soil on the ledges with Alex and Sage, her two, newest, best friends. This day has been a positive force in her path, surrounded by a group so rich in enthusiasm and support that I've felt comfortable just hanging back at times and letting her truly hike her own hike.

There are times on the way down when she is not within my sight, when my heart quickens, my thoughts race. But then I'll remember that she's with someone, the girls are always within sight of someone, and I'll settle back into the meditation of the hike.

Later, in the car, in the moments before she drifts off to sleep for the rest of the ride home, Janelle says, "I wish all people were like hiking people." The notion is sweet and childlike, but she's right, of course. Teamwork, mutual support, encouragement, working for the benefit of a common goal; that's what you do when you're at 3,500 feet and have five miles to go and darkness is coming and the ache from the previous miles has slipped into your knees and you're nearly out of Pop-Tarts.

We're all in this together.

Eastman Mtn., South Baldface, North Baldface and Eagle Crag   October 18, 2012

SUMMIT ELEVATIONS Eastman Mtn., 2,939 feet; South Baldface, 3,570 feet; North Baldface, 3,610 feet; Eagle Crag, 3,030 feet

LOCATION AND DIRECTIONS Chatham and Beans Purchase (near Evans Notch). The trailhead is located on Route 113 in Chatham, with a parking area on the east side of the road about 0.1 mi. north of the entrance to AMC's Cold River Camp.

OUR ROUTE Baldface Circle Trail to Slippery Brook Trail to Eastman Mountain Trail to Eastman summit. Backtrack down Eastman Mountain Trail to Baldface Knob back to Baldface Circle. Baldface Circle over S. and N. Baldface to Meader Trail then 0.2 to Eagle Crag. Then, backtrack down the Baldface Circle Trail to complete the loop.

TRIP MILEAGE 13 miles round trip.

IF YOU GO Maine DOT closes Route 113 through Evans Notch during the winter months. From the south, the road is open as far as the junction with the road to Basin Pond; from the north, the road is only open for the first 1.5 miles in from Route 2 in Shelburne.

| 34 |

Tower Tea Time

#41: Smarts Mountain

A raw wind whips through the broken windows of the lookout tower on Smarts Mountain. Janelle and I are forty-one feet in the air, huddled in a corner at the top of the tiny tower cab. I can feel the cab shimmy slightly in the wind. If we stick our heads up too high the wind cuts rights though our fleece like a thousand freezing knives.

While the views are spectacular from this perch, the tower, built in 1939, is not a particularly pleasant place with its graffiti and busted floor boards.

None of that appears to affect the girl in the slightest. This is the first time she's able to go inside a tower. Kearsarge. Cardigan. Magalloway. The Doublehead and Black cabins. They were all closed when we were there. But both the thru-hiker cabin below and the tower are wide open for us today, and she's in a good mood.

She shucks off her pack and begins to lay out her food and snacks with intense concentration. Janelle is not a tea party sort of girl, but this is definitely turning into a picnic, an outdoor feast at 3,200 feet, in the bitter wind, atop a dilapidated tower with gray clouds and a sleety rain spraying around us.

"Are you warm enough?" I ask as she arranges her sandwich, trail mix and apple.

She doesn't even look up. "Uh-huh. Can we have some tea?"

Exploring a unique outhouse near the summit of Smarts Mountain.

"You bet." I pull the thermos out of my pack, and as I twist it open a thick aroma of orange and ginger fills the cab.

"Yum," she says, and smiles, happily oblivious to the deluge howling around us.

It's a marvelous lunch, even though we have to keep our heads low and despite the sway of the tower.

"Can we explore the cabin as well?" she asks.

The Smarts Mountain ridge is on the Appalachian Trail, and right under the tower sits an old, well-used thru-hiker cabin. To my eye, compared to an AMC hut, this place is Blair Witch quality.

The cabin is completely bare save a stool in one corner and a crumbling table in the other. Graffiti, some of it coarse, covers the walls and porch. And the place smells like sweat and pot and mold.

But to Janelle, it is a palace, an amazing space filled with hiker history and tales of mountains. I have rarely seen her so engaged and happy as when she sits by the empty fireplace, stretches out her legs, tears off a piece of jerky and between bites declares, "We'll stay here overnight sometime, and have a fire out front and we can go up in the tower at night."

I wonder if seeing a real hut with amenities and bunk beds will change her mind, or if rustic, bare-bones spaces like this one really are her preference.

At any rate, the afternoon spins by and after a while we must head down, past the icy bog near the top and down off the slick trail rocks near the ridge.

Once off the slope of the mountain, the trail turns right and joins up with a wide and beautiful snowmobile track, and we walk cheerfully in the open woods back toward our car.

But near the bottom, a creek has broken into the trail and created a deep, wide groove of water that spills down in our path for 10 or 20 feet before seemingly disappearing into the ground.

Closer examination reveals an underground network of rock ledges where the odd erosion pattern has dropped the stream under the trail and rerouted it six feet away, where the stream continues unabated. The water in our path is due to a backup of fallen leaves in the rocky openings.

It's a small discovery, but to Janelle it might as well be stumbling upon King Tut's tomb.

She grabs a stick and is about to throw off her pack, but looks up at me first. The weather is warm, there are hours of daylight left and absolutely nothing for us to do but be here, so I just say, "Go ahead."

For the next half hour we just play—no summits, no grand views, no spectacular waterfalls. There in the golden woods, miles from any summit, Janelle and I get down on our hands and knees and get dirty. We move leaves this way and that, opening the water channels and watching in wonder as our trail dries up behind us. She sends twigs down the hole and we run to the side of the trail to watch them pop out seconds later and continue their journey downstream.

I'm tempted to turn these moments into a lesson on environmental stewardship, how the actions of just one person *can* change the natural environment, how if we can move some leaves around and change the direction of a stream, imagine what a power plant can do, or a parking lot. But I don't because I don't have to.

Being here is enough. Today we are not mountain explorers. We have no list right now. We are just two friends dipping our hands in the cold mountain stream to see what will happen.

Smarts Mountain   *October 21, 2012*

SUMMIT ELEVATION 3,238 feet

LOCATION AND DIRECTIONS Lyme. From Route 25A, 3.9 mi. east of Route 10 and Lyme village, turn right onto Quinttown Road and drive another 1.7 mi. and turn right onto Mousley Brook Road. Continue 0.7 mi., passing over a bridge and then negotiating a sharp hairpin turn to a gate. The parking area is on the left.

OUR ROUTE Daniel Doan Trail up and back.

TRIP MILEAGE 6.4 miles.

IF YOU GO The lower section of the Daniel Doan Trail passes by several camps and snowmobile trails. Be careful route-finding, in particular when you come to a double bridge. Take the right one. Mousely Brook Road may not be passable in winter so be prepared to approach the trailhead on foot from Quinttown Road.

| 35 |

Outrunning a Hurricane

> ### #42 & 43: South and North Moat Mountain

Sandy is coming.

The hurricane is expected to hit New England in 72 hours. So, as Janelle and I wind our way up the gentle slope of South Moat, I can't keep my head from calculating what remains.

The date is Oct. 27. We want to finish the list in one year, by Nov. 5. Counting today, that gives us 10 days to hike 12 mountains.

Doable, but the storm will be here in a couple days. Last year, Hurricane Irene devastated the North Country, washing out back roads and obliterating trails, permanently in some cases. If that happens this year, this quest could be over. Our goal, then, is to bring the list down to eight peaks before Sandy does whatever she will do.

Between the Moats today and Middle Sister and Chocorua tomorrow, I'll be pushing the girl to hike nearly eighteen miles in two days. It's time to see what we are really made of.

If Janelle is feeling any of this pressure, she isn't letting it show today. In the calm before the storm, the day is crystal clear and warm, the forest is quiet and as we climb up the ledges to reach South Moat and break out above treeline for good, our spirits are high and our legs are strong.

At the open summit, two young men sit enjoying the views of the surrounding valley. One of them is thrilled to see Janelle.

"Wow, how old are you?" he asks.

"Ten."

They both laugh, and one comes over to give her a high five. "I have a nephew who's just a little younger than you and we went for a little flat hike, and man, it was like I had to drag him all the way up!" He looks at me. "How do you do it?"

I shake my head. "It's all her. I'd never be able to drag her up all these mountains if she didn't want to do it."

"Mountains?" the man says and turns again to Janelle. "How many have you hiked?"

"Forty-one! No, 42 counting this one."

"Whoa," they say together and Janelle gets another round of high fives.

I stand back a little to watch this interaction, not knowing then that this exchange is the polar opposite of what we'll face tomorrow. For now, I see her grin shyly and recognize the positive effect such support has on her confidence.

With each hike, Janelle has grown and changed. She has begun to be an equal partner in this crazy quest.

It would be easy to relax all day on South Moat, but we have more than two miles of ridge walking ahead of us to North Moat, and so we bid the boys goodbye and drop down into a small col to begin the long, beautiful journey across the ridge.

This is a special place. Our trail takes us up and down through low trees and smalls hills. In some places we scramble up short ledges. In others, we stay above treeline in the sun and blue sky. From here we can see Middle Sister, Chocorua and Kearsarge North, all mountains we'll visit in the next week if Sandy allows it.

Before long, we reach a slight rise where the Red Ridge Trail turns right and heads down. We continue straight on, climb over some shining rocks and begin our final ascent of North Moat. Just below the summit, there's a thick wall of granite, which Janelle attacks ferociously.

"Come on," she yells down after scaling the ledge, "check it out."

The view from North Moat is breathtaking. The girl and I sit in the shadow of the eastern Whites and pick out places we've been. Iron. Doublehead. Black. Have we climbed all those mountains, come this far?

Tough Cookie hikes the ridge between North and South Moat.

Our shadows begin to get long and we hurry down to reach our waiting car. This has been a point-to-point hike. We left a car west of Conway at a parking area that leads to a place called Diana's Baths, a popular tourist destination. But now, as we began to lose our battle with the approaching darkness, the trail, though flat, becomes difficult.

Erosion grooves cut through and around the trail, leaving deep sitting water in our path. Leaves cover any obvious tracks. Blazes are far and few between. We have twenty minutes, tops, of daylight left.

Janelle begins to drag. I'm tired, and inexplicably my patience begins to shred. At one point, I realize she's too far behind me and I stand there, irritated, waiting for her to catch up. Despite the long day and the big miles, I know she can move faster. I *need* her to move faster, but I'm running out of ideas to motivate.

"Look ahead of us," I tell her. We are about a mile from the car, the trail is flat and we're warm. But we've already hiked nine miles, and the Moats beat both of us up. "Can you find the trail?"

She peers into the trees for a moment. "I have no idea," she grumbles.

"What will we do, here, if it gets dark?" I ask. "Imagine how much harder this will be for us."

Janelle takes a deep breath and I can see the lines of concern. She understands how important it is for us to step it up, but she's tired. There are no tears, no tween frustration. She's just tired and lowers her head.

I close my eyes for a moment and try to re-focus.

"Okay, listen," I lift her chin up. "We have headlamps, we have food. I know how strong you are. Can you hurry for the next five or ten minutes and help me find our way through all this water? Things will get better after this."

I don't know if things will get better, but she nods and offers a weak smile. "Okay." We set off into the darkening unknown.

We do make it out that night, past the beautiful rushing water of Diana's Baths, down the paved path that leads tourists to the spot, and as the last light of day leaves us we slide into the car.

I take a deep breath. "Nice job."

She smiles, but she's too tired to say anything. We have nearly nine miles and one of our most difficult days waiting for us tomorrow.

South and North Moat Mtns.   *October 27, 2012*

SUMMIT ELEVATIONS South Moat, 2,770 feet; North Moat, 3,196 feet

LOCATION AND DIRECTIONS North Conway. The southern terminus of Moat Mountain Trail is on Passaconaway Road, 3.2 miles from its intersection with West Side Road about a mile north of Conway village. Trailhead parking is on the right. The northeast terminus of the trail is found on West Side Road, 1.4 mi. north of the intersection of West Side Road and River Street to North Conway village. This is the large trailhead parking lot for popular Diana's Bath.

OUR ROUTE Moat Mountain Tail, from south to north.

TRIP MILEAGE 9.7 miles.

IF YOU GO We decided to do an end-to-end hike, which required a car spot at the other end of the ridge at the Diana's Baths parking area trailhead.

| 36 |

The Girl Comes Into Her Own

#44 & 45: Middle Sister and Mount Chocorua

On the way to our trailhead, we come across a mobile, flashing highway sign that reads: Hurricane Warnings.

I have Janelle pose in front of it for a picture.

Sandy is nearly here, the edge of this massive storm just beginning to touch New England. The air is moist and a thin overcast is sweeping up from the south. We don't have much time.

Today is Chocorua, grand Chocorua. For years, this bare, beautiful mountain has taunted me from my peripheral vision. Books and songs have been written about her.

The haunting mountain, prominent from all directions, is named after Chief Chocorua of the Pequawket tribe. Legend holds that the chief, pursued by settlers to the very top, leapt to his death after placing a curse on the white men. Darby Field himself, the first white man to touch the summit of Mount Washington, called Chocorua a "striking sentinel."

Janelle and I set off, tired from yesterday's hike and wary of the changing weather. But my stories of this mountain must have some effect: she's energetic and talkative as we make our way first to Middle Sister, Chocorua's pretty neighbor to the west, a mountain our list demands we tag.

Neither of us has many expectations about Middle Sister but we're

On the day before Hurricane Sandy, we hike the spectacular Mount Chocorua.

happily surprised when we crest the final rocky rise and see the mountain's old fire tower ruin for the first time.

In operation from 1927 to 1946, the tower was made of stone and designed to withstand the sometimes brutal and exposed nature of this ridge. Now, all that remains is the tall foundation and an eerie set of stairs to what once must have been the staircase up. Inside the four-walled foundation is what appears to be some solar-powered equipment, perhaps a weather station of some sort.

It is enchanting. With the hulking, exposed granite of Chocorua rising up to the west, we spend far more time than we should exploring beautiful Middle Sister. We sit on the foundation facing the Moats and spot ledges we hiked just the other day.

But time is short and the weather is changing. As we move off Middle Sister and begin our ascent of Chororua's enormous summit cone, a furious southern wind begins to blow and the temperature drops.

Then something wonderful happens to the girl. We pop out of treeline for the last time, and the enormous summit block of Chocorua rises before us like a granite castle, hard rock seemingly shooting straight up like gray seracs. She looks up at the open ledges and this lonely, craggy mountain seems to call out to her. Her eyes get wide and she sets her jaw to the task ahead.

The wind picks up, rolling up out of the valley below and gaining velocity as it creeps up the side of the mountain. Atop one ledge, the wind hits us and I watch her hobble for a split second before planting a pole, ducking her head and regaining her balance. She's learning how to do this, how to readjust to changing, and challenging, conditions.

She loves rock. She asks on every hike if there is any scrambling. Now, Janelle has a full quarter-mile of nearly nothing but rock exposed and sheer to play on. I work hard to keep pace.

In some areas the trail takes us up and over ledges that are eye level for her. But we work together. The wind is too loud for us to hear each other, but after forty-four mountains we know each other well enough to not need to talk. She'll toss me her poles, use her hands, then I'll toss them up to her. In one instance, she waits before climbing up a ledge and I realize she wants me to plant myself below, in case she slips.

It is a solid thirty minutes of trail dance as the girl and I duck and dodge and shimmy up this mountain, on top of the world, at the top of our game. Two months ago, she could not have done this. I would not have let her try. But now, we've reached that moment that hikers always long to feel, where the hike is effortless, where you are so in the moment with the trail that there are no aches or pains, no worries. Only joy.

We spin like this around the base of the summit rock, and she skitters ahead of me toward the summit. There, near the top, we encounter reality.

"Wow, guess you're going to be mad at your dad later for dragging you up here, huh?" The man near the summit directs his question at Janelle.

The question is so abrupt and sharp, the girl freezes. At nearly 3,500 feet in howling wind, fully exposed to the elements, I'm not interested in engaging anyone in a long explanation, so I ignore the dad part and make light of the comment. "Nah, she's the one dragging me up here. She kicked my butt all the way up!"

But he won't let it go.

"You ever been here before? First mountain?" Again, he addresses Janelle. She shakes her head no to both questions.

"We're working on the 52 With a View list, we're nearly done," I say, sidling up next to her. "Let's go find some shelter from this wind and get a bite to eat, kid-o!"

We stop at the glorious summit for a moment, then drop down to a lower rock shelf that breaks the wind. But he's not done.

"You know, if you go down the summit area about 100 yards or so," he points south, "you can find some shelter."

All I can think is that 100 yards south of the summit is no longer the summit. "We like the views," I say pleasantly.

"Great views from down there as well," he says.

"We're good. Thanks." I put an edge to my tone, which he appears to hear, as he doesn't bother us again. And soon, there are half a dozen other hikers at the summit and we're forgotten.

Janelle and I lean back against the rocks and sip chicken noodle soup out of a thermos, and all is again right with the world. After a little while, she says, "That guy, there was something wrong with him."

"Guess he was a little creepy, huh? I'm sorry if he ruined your hike."

"Why would he do that?" She turns back to her snacks, and under her breath says, "Just there was something wrong with *him*, that's all."

A hiking friend of mine once suggested that for some adults, after spending hours huffing and puffing their way up a mountain, seeing a child at the top deflates their own sense of accomplishment. Bursts their bubble, so to speak. We've been lucky, Janelle and I, surrounded by family and friends and a hiking community that is genuinely enthusiastic and encouraging about our quest.

And now, as we sit at the top of Chocorua with the waves of wind from approaching Hurricane Sandy bursting like tiny explosions over the mountain's bald top, the end is in sight.

If all goes well and Sandy causes no harm, we'll tag the summit of Starr King next week, together, and then . . . what?

I watch my partner out of the corner of my eye as she deliberately shovels soup into her mouth, her eyes never wavering from the long view.

"What are you thinking?" I ask.

She shrugs, never turning from the view. "This is my favorite."

The mountain? The soup? The view? I don't ask. It's her favorite and that's enough.

Middle Sister and Mt. Chocorua   *October 28, 2012*

SUMMIT ELEVATIONS Middle Sister, 3,340 feet; Mt. Chocorua, 3,500 feet

LOCATION AND DIRECTIONS Albany (off Kancamagus Highway). The Champney Falls Trail is found off the Kancamagus Highway (Route 112), 11.5 mi. west of Route 16 in Conway. Trail parking is on the south side of the road.

OUR ROUTE Champney Falls Trail to Middle Sister Cutoff to Middle Sister, then the Middle Sister Trail to Piper Trail to summit. On the return, straight down the Champney Falls Trail.

TRIP MILEAGE 8.1 miles.

IF YOU GO The summit of Chocorua can be reached from all sides, via many trails. One of the most popular is the Piper Trail from Route 16 south of Conway. Because of its low elevation and reputation, many beginners hike Chocorua and deeply underestimate how difficult the mountain is in many places. Do your homework, and treat Chocorua with added respect.

| 37 |

Defeat, of a Sort

#46: Mount Paugus

True, in retrospect our goal for this hike was laughably ambitious: a complete loop through the Sandwich Range Wilderness designed to encompass three more peaks on our list, Paugus, Square Ledge and Hibbard. After those three, we'd burn through the remaining five and finish on November 8, not exactly one year from the day of our start, but close enough.

And yes, this was to be our longest hike, nearly 14 miles. And fine, we didn't have nearly as much daylight for such a hike, and it was only two days after Hurricane Sandy laid waste to some parts of the White Mountains.

But still. We are strong. We've hiked in rain and ice. We can taste the finish.

How were we to know that our entire one-year goal would be up-ended by little Whitin Brook? Sandy's deluge has swollen this little brook into a majestic river. I just stand there looking at the thing, the roar of water almost too loud to speak over. This would normally be a hop across, a one-boot jump. Today, we cannot get across.

The day started well enough. We hit the Big Rock Cave Trail early enough, spent a few minutes checking out the caves, and climbed up and over Mount Mexico in good time. Now, Paugus awaits, and Whitin Brook will not let us pass.

We take off our packs and I move first downstream, then up. Nothing. The brook is not wide, or even very deep. But the water rushes violently and is cold. One slip and the hike is over. We'd have no choice but to go back.

Janelle picks up some tree branches and drags them to the side of the brook, but as she attempts to bridge the water gap, the current simply snatches them out of her hands and shoves the trees downstream.

"We're gonna get wet," she says sadly.

Indeed. But not in the way she imagines. We've now spent twenty minutes trying to figure this out and I've had enough.

"Janelle, either we go or we don't. Enough messing around. Take off your boots."

There's a long pause as she considers this curious and unexpected development. She's never forded water before. "But the water is cold."

"Yup."

"Our feet will get cold."

"Only a little, then we'll warm them up."

"What if I fall in?"

"We turn around and go home, but you won't fall in."

I find a narrow and reasonably flat section of the brook where the water doesn't seem too fast. I can do this in three steps, maybe. She'll need more. We pull out our fleece and heavy coats. I want us to be as warm as possible as we cross. I sit her down at the place of our crossing.

"Boots off, and socks," I say. "Tuck your socks into the boots, then I'm going to tie your boots around your neck so they stay dry. Once our boots are off, we'll move quick, use our poles, you follow me exactly. We'll get to the other side, dry off our feet fast and get the socks and boots back on."

"Really?"

"Our boots will be off for five minutes, tops."

And so we do. Packs unbuckled, boots around our necks, baby steps upstream. The water is very cold and rushes fast over my ankles. The water is nearly up to her knees.

My left hand holds her right and we step together into the frigid water. I see my toes go white almost immediately and momentarily consider turning around, but she's on the move and it's too late for backtracking.

"It's freezing!" she shouts, half in terror and half laughing.

We take two steps together and the current pushes hard. I feel the rush push her back, but pull against it holding her tightly. We take three steps, then four and five before stepping onto the opposite shore.

"Great job!" I say.

I sit her down and damp-dry her feet with paper towels and slide her socks back on. Once her boots are on, I say, "Go walk around now, jump up and down and you'll be fine in a minute."

In a few minutes she's skipping around the shore. "I did it, I crossed a river barefoot!"

This teamwork is a great moment of triumph for us. A new obstacle vanquished, another building block for her confidence and a story to tell her grandmother.

In the back of my head, I still have a vague sense that we could salvage this day, tag the summits we came here to tag.

But after a difficult climb up the Paugus cliff, I understand that we are done.

There is no getting around the blowdowns. Four hours into our hike, with miles to go, Janelle and I are faced with a seemingly impossible-to-solve puzzle. We are now too far into the hike to turn around, especially since going back would require a steep descent off the Paugus cliff. But ahead of us the trail is destroyed.

Hurricane Sandy has left a swath of destruction and we're now in the middle of the wreckage. The Old Paugus Trail, in this section, is gone, as though the hand of a giant has swished across the range, brushing over four- and five-inch-thick trees like toothpicks. I cannot see the continuation of the trail on the other side of the enormous, perhaps valley-wide, blowdown.

"What do we do?" Janelle asks. I sense her frustration, and feel my own. It has already been a tiring hike. The day is raw and windy. Three summits is now out of the question. Finishing in one year's time is impossible.

We take the opportunity to explore Big Rock Caves on the way up Mount Paugus.

But even more disturbing is the problem immediately facing us in the form of what appears to be the obliteration of the trail.

I slip off my pack and gulp down some water. Then, I push on the cluster of fallen trees in front of us, checking for give. There is none, which is good. It means the blowdown directly in front at least is fully down and won't collapse on us.

"Take off your pack," I say. "We have to create a path."

The slope to our right is too steep to go down and back around, and the up-slope to our left is too dangerous to attempt. So the girl and I slowly begin snapping off branches on the trees in our path, trying to create a window among the trunks. That's grueling work. After a while we have enough of an opening to slip through. We zig and zag in and out and under the trees, snapping branches in some places, crawling on our hands and knees in others, until an opening appears ahead.

After thirty minutes of work we step through onto the path and come face to face with another, bigger, section of blowdown. And beyond that, more.

"Well, at least if anybody hikes this after us, they'll have an easier time," Janelle says.

"Yup. Let's get to work."

An hour later, we chop and cut and break our way to the Paugus summit ledges, exhausted and frustrated. From here, we can look across the valley toward Square Ledge and Hibbard and our proposed trail home, but it's too late in the day and we're too bone-tired to try for such a loop.

Janelle finds a split rock on a ledge and sinks into it like an easy chair. She puts her feet up, leans back and lounges. I can't help but laugh, and soon we're both laughing, through our disappointment and through our sudden understanding that finishing a week later, or two weeks later, is still finishing.

"Can we have a party after we're done?" Janelle says.

"Oh, heck yes!" I say and join her on her little rock throne. We're cold and the sky is gray and raw, but we crouch down under cover of the rock and share some cookies, and like it usually does in the mountains, the wind carries our worries away.

Mt. Paugus

SUMMIT ELEVATION 3,198 feet

LOCATION AND DIRECTIONS Albany (though trailhead is actually in
   Tamworth). From junction of Routes 113 and 113A in Tamworth
   village, take 113A north to Wonalancet settlement. The parking lot and
   trailhead are on the right about a half mile east of the sharp left turn
   at Wonalancet. The alternate route is to follow Route 113 east from
   Holderness through Center Sandwich and then North Sandwich. Turn
   north here onto Route 113A and continue to Wonalancet and the above
   mentioned sharp turn. The trail is on your left in this direction.

OUR ROUTE Cabin Trail to Big Rock Cave Trail to Old Paugus Trail to
   Lawrence Trail then back to Cabin Trail, loop.

TRIP MILEAGE 8.4 miles.

IF YOU GO This was not our originally planned loop, but it's a fine one in and
   of itself. The Big Rock Caves are a fine, fun family destination and easily
   reached.

Getting a Ten-Year-Old Girl Comfortable
with "Going" in the Woods

On our very first hike, pre–52 With a View, Janelle was unable to relieve herself in the woods. Near the end of that thankfully short hike, we spent a fairly desperate ten minutes frantically searching for a nearby outhouse and barely made it there in time.

I'm no expert on ten-year-olds, kids, bathroom etiquette . . . oh, let's just face it, I'm not an expert on anything. But, I do know that if you're going to hike ten miles, at some point, you have to go to the bathroom.

The first few times, Meena went into the woods with Janelle. But ultimately, if you are a middle-aged man hiking with a ten-year-old girl, that kid is going to have to learn to go to the bathroom alone.

So, what to do?

Guys have it easy: First, remember that guys both big and little can pretty much go wherever they want. And unless it happens to be in the middle of the street, they can go with impunity. Basically, guys can just turn their backs, find a tree, and take care of things. Girls, not so much.

Compare and contrast: One way that helped Janelle be more comfortable with the woods as a bathroom was to show her outhouses, which are nearly universally worse than finding a tree. The kid is also a runner and since port-a-potties at races are apocalyptic in their appearance, she quickly understood that going in the woods was a superior option.

Things won't bite or attack you any more or less than they normally would just because your pants are down: Believe it or not, this is a tough lesson. I mean your bottom is showing, why wouldn't a bee or snake choose that exact moment to bite or sting you? After a few hikes, Janelle understood that peeing in the woods attracted bears no more or no less than walking in the woods.

Take your time, respect the discomfort: Yes, fine, they have squat toilets in Asia. But not here. And we have branches, and mushrooms and inclines to contend with. And poison ivy. So, depending on the terrain, it takes a little hunting to find the perfect spot. One of Janelle's biggest fears early on was that once she found a spot, she wouldn't be able to find her way back. This meant that I would march into the woods with her, we'd find a good spot for her, then I'd march back (but not out of earshot) and she'd call when she was done so I could come get her. Slowly, I weaned her off this cumbersome process and she learned to do it on her own.

Empowerment: Yes, even in something as primal and icky, girl power can play a role. Think about it. After a little practice, here's something girls can do just as well as boys. In fact, "going" in the woods became just another badge of toughness, of being able to do the kind of hikes and climb the kind of mountains that many of her peers could not. After all the mud, fungus, animal scat, snow, bruises and blood, a mountain bathroom break can be downright relaxing.

| 38 |

Escaping Winter, for Now

#48: Kearsarge North

Winter is afoot.

Near the top of Kearsarge North, on the outskirts of North Conway, we begin to see and feel signs that we are not going to escape winter before we finish the list.

We changed our plans at the last moment this morning, heading south of the notches to escape a full-on winter storm raging in the North Country. We wanted to head to Shelburne Moriah near Gorham today to get that difficult climb behind us, but I wasn't going to risk that hike in storm conditions. Plus, we were beat up from yesterday's Paugus blowdown fiasco.

The moment we crested the highpoint at Crawford Notch near the Highland Center and began the downward drive toward Conway, the weather nearly instantly cleared. It was still very cold, but at least we didn't need to face snow. Yet.

The lower sections of the Kearsarge North Trail were bare and dry. But here, above 3,000 feet, pockets of hail and ice mark the trail. We pause before the exposed ledges, our breath short and visible. I'm feeling chilled here, and above us a cold wind roars over the summit and we can hear trees groan under its force.

"Layer up, kid-o," I say. "Full-on winter conditions. Get your fleece on and your jacket on top of that."

Janelle immediately drops her pack and starts rummaging around for her gear. No protest. Questions will come later. We're fully a team now. In the last few weeks as we've inched closer to the finish line, I've been humbled by her trust.

The Chocorua hike was a turning point for us, the moment when this child became a hiker, began to understand her environment and her capabilities, not as an adult, but in an adult way. I watch her gear up on her own because she understands now what she must do to stay safe and warm.

"Can we have some tea before we go up there?" she asks. This simple treat of warmth and comfort has become a ceremony of sorts for us, a way to prepare for a difficulty ahead and as a way to celebrate and relax after a challenge.

So I break out the thermos and my partner and I sip raspberry tea, pull our hats down over our brows and listen to the wind scream above us. Full-on winter conditions. This will be our first foray into cold like that.

"Listen," I say, casually as though it's no big deal. "It's going to be cold up there like we haven't felt before, so we need to stay close and listen to each other. If you feel anything getting too cold, you tell me right away, okay?"

She nods. I give her cheek a pat with my gloved hand. "Let's go."

She smiles and hits the ledges at nearly a run. The freezing wind waits.

There is nothing like the clarity of a frigid summit. We break out above treeline and bee-line to the mountain's newly remodeled observation tower. We feel like pampered hikers here. An observation tower is not needed, as the summit itself is open and wide and the chilled air provides spectacular views in all directions.

But today, as we duck against the force of winter gusts that threaten to pick Janelle up and fling her into the valley, the tower is a wonderful retreat. Recently remodeled, the tower sits lower than normal fire towers, only about fifteen feet up, making the climb to the observation deck less intimidating. The tower is surrounded by long windows

Taking the time for some play at the summit of Kearsarge North.

on all four sides. This feature creates a greenhouse effect inside, and as Janelle and I step out of the wind into the main cab, our glasses fog over and we are able to strip down to just our base layer.

There are half a dozen hikers in the wide cab, so Janelle and I tuck ourselves out of the way into a far corner to eat lunch, where we sit back and people watch. There are a couple of women, each working on the 52 list as well, and their eyes go wide when I mention this is No. 47 for Janelle. There, a solo woman who passed us on the way up works Janelle into a lather with tales of "ice skiing," where a regular ski slope is transformed into an ice slope that skaters with specially designed skis can sail down. We relax and chat until another solo hiker comes in, strips off nearly all his clothes, and pulls a bottle of beer out of his pack. Janelle and I look at each other; it's our cue to leave.

The wind appears to have died down some, but as we look north beyond the notches, we can see the storm is still raging. Tomorrow will be interesting.

There's still a fair amount of construction material and debris from the remodel at the summit, and before we leave Janelle asks if she can take down a small block of wood, nearly a perfect square about the size of a Rubik's Cube. There are some numbers on one side written in thick black marker, likely a carpenter's scribbles to help determine where that piece of lumber would go.

"Why do you want it?" I ask.

She shrugs. "It's pretty."

The wood is also junk that will at some point be carted away by the Forest Service, so I let her have it, thinking that it will be forgotten in no time.

But later that evening as we relax at the cabin, eating pasta off plastic plates, she takes the cube out of her pack and puts it on the table between us. She moves the numbers so they face her.

"Our table setting," she says happily.

Kearsarge North   *November 4, 2012*

SUMMIT ELEVATION 3,268 feet

LOCATION AND DIRECTIONS Bartlett (though summit is technically in Chatham). The trailhead is located on the north side of Hurricane Mountain Road, which leaves Route 16 opposite the state highway rest area and scenic vista in Intervale, just outside North Conway village. Follow Hurricane Mountain Road approximately 1.5 miles, where there is a small parking area on the left.

OUR ROUTE Mt. Kearsarge North Trail, up and back.

TRIP MILEAGE 6.2 miles.

IF YOU GO The fire tower atop Kearsarge North has the distinction of being open to the public year-round, and hikers and backpackers can stay overnight there at no cost. Be forewarned, during the summer season it may get crowded, but during the winter the tower provides a unique opportunity to capture amazing winter sunsets in relative safety and warmth as long as you have a good sleeping bag.

| 39 |

We Climb, It's What We Do

> ### #48: The Horn

When we step onto the Unknown Pond Trail and begin our trek to The Horn, flakes are falling gently. One hour later, it is snowing and we are in three inches of fluff. By the time we reach Unknown Pond and the trail junction toward The Horn, we still have nearly two miles to go, the temperature has dropped to well below freezing, and the snow and sleet come down hard in giant icy drops.

Above us, over the trees, we can see clouds shooting by under a stiff, cold wind.

It is winter. The Horn is nearly a 4,000-footer. We are deep into the remote Kilkenny Ridge of New Hampshire's North Country, far from any comfort zone. I should be worried, and yet as I watch the girl chow down some trail mix and tighten her boots, snowflakes piling up on her shoulders, I feel fairly calm.

We've worked hard to be here, and we know each other well. When I ask her to pose for a shot next to the trail sign, she crosses her arms and puts one leg up, a pose. She smiles widely and I resist asking for the millionth time if she's warm enough. Clearly she is.

The snowy trail swings us around Unknown Pond and the draw of water is too great for her to resist. We take a short path off trail down to the shore and look out across the remote pond, iced thinly with a dusty coating of snow over the top.

"I've never seen an ice pond," she says. I hold her hand as she crouches down to touch the thin ice, too thin to walk over yet.

We visit Unknown Pond on the way to The Horn, seen here in the background.

Soon, we are slowly heading up. The trail approaches The Horn from the mountain's western flank and swings us around the outside first, before turning left and attacking the slope directly. And as we hike, the snow gets deeper and the trail becomes slicker.

Incredibly, Janelle is still wearing her Walmart trail runners. We've added thicker socks and gaiters to the mix to afford some protection from the snow, but I'm amazed her feet remain warm in those things.

Once we begin the approach to The Horn's small but unique summit, the treeline thins and it gets colds fast. The final thirty yards to the top are slippery, steep rock climbs and the snow is not yet deep enough to walk atop the ice. We pick our way carefully up, but just below the summit I begin to feel an instinctive sense of danger, a feeling that doing it this way is not quite right.

"Kid-o," I say, "hold up. We need to get better prepared for this."

I have her gear fully up, including snow pants and traction on her feet in the form of devices called Stabilicers. They are hard rubber soles with metal screws in the bottom that strap onto the bottom of her boots. We are now close enough to the summit to be able to leave our packs and poles behind. I want us to be as mobile as possible up there, and it turns out I'm right.

The Horn has a unique distinction. The mountain's summit is one very large, very steep rock. In the summer, a hiker can scramble up that rock from several different points. Now, however, as we attain the summit, we hover helplessly around the summit rock. Those icy flanks might as well be Mount Everest.

We explore the base of the summit rock for ten minutes, fully exposed to a bitter valley wind, our sweat freezing to our fleece. We are seven feet from the top, but that's seven feet up a rock face and our Stabilicers are not up to the task.

If we reach up with our poles we can touch the summit. But it looks like our feet aren't going to make it.

And time begins to run out.

"We've been here too long, Janelle," I say close to her ear, over the howl of cold wind. "It's too dangerous."

I could, I suppose, heave her up there. But then how would I get her down?

"We'll have to come back!" She says this not as a statement or question, but as a dreaded exclamation. Neither of us wants to miss a summit. We won't have enough time to come back. It's now or nothing.

"Are you warm, every part of you, are you warm?" I ask.

"Yes."

There is one chance. The western side of the giant boulder is split near the bottom, forming a wedge about two feet wide and ten feet long. I have no clue what's on the other side of that wedge. Perhaps more impossible-to-negotiate rock. Perhaps a pathway to the top. "Can you fit through there?" I know she can fit. My question is designed to see if she wants to.

"Yes!" she says again, nodding her head to add emphasis. There's no hesitation, no claustrophobic fear. She's excited.

"Okay," I say. "Let's take one last shot. Follow me. Do as I do. If I say turn back, we just shimmy back the way we came, okay?"

And so, at nearly 4,000 feet, amid the ice and snow, fully engaged and ready for anything, the girl and I squeeze into the void to search for a path to the summit.

I lean into the rock, skittering on my elbows and knees. She does the same but her size makes it much easier for her. At the other side of

Our first winter views are from the top of The Horn.

the split, beyond a small tree, the summit rock appears to slope down enough for us to climb up onto it.

"What do you see?" Janelle asks.

"I think we can do this," I say. "Let me look before you try it, okay?"

I crawl on my hands and knees to get under and around the tree, the slope to my left dangerously steep. Once at the base of the rock, I brace my foot on that same tree and am indeed able to get up on the rock.

She follows, and I hold her hand as she wheels around the tree and comes up the side of the rock. But we have one last challenge. Incredibly, near the top, that rock is tiered and the actual summit is still four feet up a shelf.

With the wind howling in my ears, and sleet stinging my eyes, I boost myself up to the top, then turn around.

"Jump!"

Even in the crazy urgency of the moment, she gives me a look. THE look. I have come to understand this particular expression not as annoyance, but something approaching chagrin. It is the look equivalent to rolling her eyes that demands I stop taking pictures or quit making bad jokes or lets me know that I am stark raving mad if I think she's is going to jump four feet up in swirling snow and ice at nearly 4,000 feet. That's a look I can only imagine scores of young men will receive in years to come.

"We're here, you wanted adventure!" I yell over the turmoil. "You wanted to be a mountain climber. Here it is. Right now!"

Our eyes meet through the snow and the corners of her mouth lift slightly.

"Jump! Jump now!"

She crouches below me as low as she can, and grinds her feet into the snow for traction. I get to my knees, find purchase on the cold rock below, bend down toward her and reach out my arms.

She jumps; a moment of slowed time as she comes into my arms and I find two solid handfuls of her coat and her upward momentum throws us back where we land together, safe, on the summit.

The roar of the wind and the cold of the snow returns as we untangle and lift our arms to the sky there atop The Horn.

"That," she says between adrenaline-soaked breaths, "was awesome!"

The Horn
November 5, 2012

SUMMIT ELEVATION   3,905 feet

LOCATION AND DIRECTIONS   Kilkenny Township (south of Stark). From Route 110, 0.5 mi. east of Stark village, turn south onto Mill Brook Road and drive 4.5 mi. to the end of the gravel road. The trail begins just east of the bridge over Mill Brook.

OUR ROUTE   Unknown Pond Trail to Kilkenny Ridge Trail to The Horn Spur, out and back.

TRIP MILEAGE   8.4 miles.

IF YOU GO   Mill Pond Road is not maintained in the winter. There is nothing like The Horn anywhere in the Whites. At less than a hundred feet under a 4,000-footer, this hike and climb is every bit as challenging as many much higher mountains. Even in summer, prepare for long miles and difficult conditions. Few summits offer such a challenge and few offer such rewards.

| 40 |

A Moment Worth the Whole Adventure

#49: Shelburne Moriah

The mountain gods are merciful today, a gift perhaps for all our hard work the weeks before. The wicked *sturm und drang* of the past few days is gone, replaced by a soothing calm, the winter landscape of a quiet mountain at rest.

Reaching Shelburne Moriah is a long hike in a far northeast corner of the White Mountains, and we move slowly, our muscles sore, clothes filthy from three previous difficult hikes in a row.

If there is a single moment to take away from this whole journey, it is this one. We are alone, sailing along the Shelburne Moriah ridge, two travelers moving through the spectacular landscape, our breath strong, legs sure. Our Stabilicers clack comfortably on the frozen granite. The wind is slight, the sky deep blue.

The girl moves ahead of me, as always, a small pink and red form. She rarely needs help with directions now. The early first hikes where she'd agonize over blazes or get frustrated at trail markers are long behind her. She sees like a hiker now. I watch her shift her poles this way or that, pausing nearly imperceptibly occasionally to seek out the next yellow slash or twist in the trail.

Her movement is regulated and purposeful.

Above treeline, the blazes or cairns are what guide us as we wind

Making quick work of the bog bridges along the ridge of Shelburne Moriah.

our way toward the summit of Shelburne Moriah. The day has already been long and we both know we won't make it back to our car before dark, but it doesn't matter today.

We climb up a small hump and come to a vast clearing and Janelle does stop there. "Is that the summit?" she asks, pointing ahead to an outcropping maybe a quarter-mile away.

"I think so," I say. "I've never been here so I don't know if that's a false summit or not. But it seems right."

She shrugs. It makes no difference to her, or me, here, in this place above the clouds. She spins fully around, taking in the deep views and the soft white snow coating the pines. To our immediate west, Moriah and the Carters roll pleasantly in the shadow of the northern Presidentials.

"That's Mount Washington," I say and point with my walking stick to the Northeast's highest point. The air is so clear we can see the tips of the observatory and summit buildings glimmering like diamonds. Janelle studies Mt. Washington for a while, tilting her head as though she's about to say something. But she keeps it inside. I wonder how long I have before we'll be headed there. Next summer, maybe?

On the ridge, the trails drops us in and out of the trees, through beautiful frozen dells where evergreens drip white and yesterday's wind has sculpted snow into crisp, unusual shapes. We walk across wooden bog bridges as slick as ice and over sitting water now frozen a shade of blue so deep it looks nearly black in the sun.

We top out, rise after rise, with each mini-summit affording us views better than the last. Finally, we come upon a large cairn, our summit amidst what seems like an entire ridge worth of summits.

"This is it." Janelle says. It's a statement, but she still looks at me for confirmation. I nod.

She tucks herself against the cairn to get out of the wind. It's an automatic action. The wind is neither particularly strong nor that cold.

I sit next to her and we snack for a bit, saying nothing, thinking everything. I don't need to tell her how wonderful this place is. She knows. She doesn't need to let me know she's warm and happy. I know.

I search for a word to encompass this summit and remember something the Dalai Lama said, that since he believed that, at heart, human beings are gentle so too should humans' attitudes toward nature be gentle.

"Gentle," I say out loud.

"What?" Janelle asks.

"It's gentle up here."

She nods and we sit for a spell on this gentle mountain, and the day is one without worry, a day when we have come together fully in a place that has cauterized our love of hiking and of being with each other.

Shelburne Moriah   *November 6, 2012*

SUMMIT ELEVATION 3,735 feet

LOCATION AND DIRECTIONS Shelburne. The trailhead for the Rattle River Trail is on Route 2, 3.5 mi. east of the junction of Routes 2 and 16 in Gorham. Parking is available in a small lot near the east end of the bridge over Rattle River, about 300 yards east of the intersection with North Road.

OUR ROUTE Rattle River Trail to Kenduskeag Trail to summit, out and back.

TRIP MILEAGE 11.2 miles.

IF YOU GO Shelburne Moriah can also be reached from the Wild River near

Evans Notch. There is no short route to this little-hiked mountain, but reaching the summit is ample reward for such a long hike. The Rattle River Trail to the ridge is also a link in the Appalachian Trail, and Rattle River Shelter, a three-sided lean-to, is only about two miles in from Route 2.

| 41 |

Break on Through

#50 & 51: Square Ledge and Hibbard Mountain

Our penultimate hike is taxing.

Try as we might, neither of us can shake the doldrums. We're nearly finished. Even as we hike, arrangements are being made to celebrate the conclusion of our quest tomorrow. Friends and family will gather at our cabin and, after what we hope to be an easy hike up Mount Starr King, we'll share in the amazing journey with all the people who helped make it happen.

There will be a cake. Janelle's wonderful and creative aunt Nancy has created a marzipan hiker Janelle to decorate the cake, though Janelle does not know this yet. What she does know is that friends will be there and all the moments of struggle will bloom into joy and celebration.

For now though, we drag. The weather is raw and wet. The snow is sticky and even with Stabilicers our feet get sucked in like we're walking through white quicksand. This more than nine-mile hike with limited views through the Sandwich Range Wilderness is leaving us ragged and surly.

Still, this is it. I selfishly turned down offers from hiker friends to make this traverse with us. I wanted Janelle to myself. Tomorrow will be a victory lap, filled with family and friends. Today, I want to share this one final hike with Janelle as we began, the two of us moving through the wilderness, learning, exploring, bonding.

But we are tired and mostly just want to get it done.

Square Ledge is first, and the sharp, steep climb up to the plateau of this "mountain" leaves us breathless. Technically, Square Ledge, like a few other summits on the list, is a ledge of another mountain, in this case of 4,000-footer Mount Passaconaway. At the top, deep, unbroken snow and blowdowns left over from last week's storm prevent us from enjoying any real views, though we do manage to find a couple of partial outlooks.

We march on, interested now in the end, not the journey.

Our path sweeps us down off Square Ledge and back up an eastern slope of Passaconaway. Janelle and I play mind games and count out our steps in the snow. This section of the trail is less than a mile to a junction that will turn us toward Hibbard, but the climb seems to last all day.

"I don't know if I can do this," Janelle says halfway up.

I smile and sit down in the snow next to her. There we rest for a long fifteen minutes, sipping water and eating cold chocolate. There's no longer any need for morale boosting. She knows we're not turning around. But this break does serve the purpose of refocusing my energy, of turning my attention back to my partner and our bond and the sad understanding that this journey is winding down.

"We have one more summit," I say gently. "Then, we climb with the girls and then we party."

The ridge to Hibbard is long and endless, and once there we find only one small lookout. We snap pictures almost on automatic pilot, and climb down the southern side of the mountain into the upper valley and begin our final march out. Like the Moats, we left my car at Ferncroft parking area to give us no option but to make it all the way through.

It occurs to me, as we leave the Hibbard summit, that I have finished my list. Hibbard was No. 52; I have climbed them all. But as I watch this child in front of me weave authoritatively into the valley I understand this accomplishment means nothing without her. Only tomorrow, as we touch a summit I've been to half a dozen times, will this quest mean anything to me. Only then.

Square Ledge offers few lookouts and we are getting eager to finish our journey.

Finally, still a mile from the end, as the ache in our legs grows, something happens. Darkness falls. The conditions force us to slow down, to concentrate and go inward as we search for blazes and work to stay on trail. In the black of the night our headlamps illuminate only each other and we begin to remember the real reason we're here, the real reason we've done this for one full year.

"I smell campfire," Janelle says.

"Woodstove," I say. "We must be getting close to the trailhead."

"Oh," she says. Do I detect a hint of melancholy?

Finally, ten hours after we begin, we are at the car, bedraggled, hungry and cold. The Ferncroft parking area and trailhead sits right at the head of a vast farm field, the nearest house hundreds of yards away behind a grove of trees. There is no light, and the sky is winter clear.

We pull the thermos of soup out of my pack, bundle up and sit on the back bumper to eat.

"Turn off your headlamp for a second," I say.

There at the end of our personal journey, sipping soup, her legs dangling off the ground, in below-freezing weather, the girl looks up at the sky for a long time. The stars this night are so clear and brilliant, the Milky Way is a bright streak of white, like an artist dragged a paint brush across the sky.

There is nothing and everything at once. It is like she and I are alone at the foot of the universe.

I fight the urge to speak, to tell her about the stars, to congratulate her on this accomplishment, to let her know how terribly proud I am of her. I have so much to say to her.

"I've never seen so many stars," she says instead, saving me from ruining the moment. "Can we stay here a little longer?"

"As long as you like."

She nods, and sips soup and stares up at the heavens, and we stay there in the cold just a little bit longer.

Square Ledge and Hibbard Mtn.   *November 10, 2012*

SUMMIT ELEVATIONS Square Ledge, 2,620 feet; Hibbard Mtn., 2,940 feet

LOCATION AND DIRECTIONS Albany. The trailhead for Oliverian Brook Trail is on a gravel road off the south side of the Kancamagus Highway, 1.0 mi. west of Bear Notch Road. As this was a through-hike of sorts, we had a second vehicle spotted at the Ferncroft area of Wonalancet on Route 113A in Tamworth.

OUR ROUTE Oliveria Brook Trail to Square Ledge Branch Trail to Square Ledge Trail to Passaconaway Cutoff to Walden Trail to Wonalancet Range Trail to Ferncroft.

TRIP MILEAGE 9.6 miles.

IF YOU GO There are many ways and many routes to take to tackle both or each of these mountains, including several loop hikes and some overnight variations. This area of the Sandwich Range Wilderness is rugged and beautiful and includes several peaks, some of which are 4,000-footers. Find an AMC topo map, look it over, and spend some time exploring these woods.

| 42 |

Beautiful Journey

#52: Mount Starr King

Be sure of the foundation of your life.
Know why you live as you do.
Be ready to give a reason for it.
— THOMAS STARR KING

On November 11, 2012, one year and six days since we began our journey, we pull into the Starr King parking lot and Janelle is frantically greeted by her hiking friends.

No sooner does she step out of the car than she's swamped by Alex and Sage in a smothering greeting of giddy hugs and cheerful "Congratulations!"

"Wow, what a way to start, wish people were that happy to see me," says our friend Steve. It's been months since he hiked with us, and we are thrilled to have him along for our final climb.

I go over and give Trish a hug. "The girls are a little excited," she says. "Me too," I say.

Meena, alas, is not with us today, but her job today is actually far more important than this hike. She's preparing a celebration at the cabin. Even as Janelle and I gear up for our last hike of the list, friends and family of Janelle are making their way north to where Meena awaits, prepping and baking for a party. All we have to do to earn it is climb one more little mountain.

I manage to pull Janelle out of earshot of the others for a moment.

Pausing for a picture at the beginning of our final hike.

I had a little speech prepared, but I can't remember most of it, so instead I just say, "I want you to remember this day. I want you to remember the trail, how you feel, who you're with, what you experience. Forget about the past year and forget about what's next. Just be here in the moment, with me, today. Can you do that?"

"I'll try," she says. "Yes."

And with that we're off—us six wanderers—the three girls in the lead, of course. They set a powerful pace, a potent mix of excitement and joy driving them up Starr King's mild slope.

In short order we pass by the stone foundation ruins of an old spring-house. All that remains now is a circular stone wall which looks like a dried up well. The girls gather around and explore the ruins a bit. A small house was usually built over such springs and used for cold storage or to protect the water source from the elements.

I always wondered why Thomas Starr King wasn't more prominent in White Mountain lore, considering the impact of his book, *The White Hills; their Legends, Landscape and Poetry*. Published in 1859 at a time when Starr King was pastor of Hollis Street Church in Boston, the book was wildly successful and is credited as the engine that led to the modern tourism industry in the White Mountains. For more than a decade, Starr King vacationed in the Whites and explored the area, including a climb up Mount Washington, at a time when the North Country was still untamed and few dared to venture into the hills.

Now, 153 years after that book was published, Janelle and I conclude our own journey here, on the mountain named for him, in the place that Starr King, literally, put on the map.

The trail swings right and begins to attack the mountain from the southwest, and as we get higher, the snow gets deeper and the day gets warmer. The girls chat and hike, and chat and eat, and chat and rest, and we adults work hard to keep up and make sure they are warm and comfortable. Doing so is made more difficult as we swing west again and duck into heavy tree cover. The warm day melts the snow off the evergreens and as we climb higher and higher the cold snow coming off the trees makes it feel like it's raining, and we become chilled quickly.

Less than a mile from the summit, we all make the decision to get rain gear on the girls, so we stop and Janelle wraps up and we snack for the final push.

"How you doing?" I ask.

"Good," she says, then adds, "I'm warm and full, though I think I'll have a drink."

I appreciate that she's now able to recognize my concerns and head them off ahead of time.

We continue on up. As we make the final turn toward the summit, Trish whispers in my ear. "We didn't bring poles, I need your poles for the summit."

So we stop again, one last time, and Janelle and I hand off our poles to our friends.

"Let's give them a few minutes, Janelle," I say as the rest of our party heads up without us.

We stand alone then, just below the summit of Starr King with only 100 feet left to conclude our quest. Wet snow drips like rain from the branches above us. Steam rises from our clothes.

Janelle walks under the hiker pole arch atop Mount Starr King, the traditional summit welcome for a hiker who has just completed a list.

"What are they doing?" Janelle asks.

"They're putting together a special summit welcome for you."

"Cool!"

There's too much to say to her. After more than a year, after all this quest has cost us, after all we've grown and changed, to be steps away is nearly too much to bear. She is bursting with energy; jittery, unable to stand still.

I only have a few seconds, but I simply cannot form the right words.

So, I get down on my knees in the snow, and turn her toward me. She's smiling, icy snow dripping off her eyelashes, cheeks beet red. I pull my hiking partner to me and hug her. With gloves and over full packs, the hug feels clumsy. Snow sitting atop our shoulders and hats runs down our backs, but I hold on for a little too long and thankfully she lets me.

I straighten up and take a deep breath. "This is it."

"Yup."

"How do you feel?"

"Good!"

I pause and she looks at me, waiting to be released. "Okay, go get it . . ."

My Spider Monkey and I celebrate the end of one journey and the beginning of another at the old cabin fireplace atop Starr King.

Tough Cookie turns back to the trail and forges ahead, confident, strong and sure; my powerful spider monkey moves away from me and up into the sun.

I follow, an emotional mess, and within minutes, the trail tops out and we round a turn to find our friends at the summit. They use our poles to form an arch for Janelle to walk beneath, the traditional welcome to the final summit for a hiker who has completed a mountain list. They applaud and cheer as Tough Cookie takes her final steps and walks confidently under the poles, a wide grin on her face, her eyes speaking volumes about the depth and authority she now commands.

At the summit is an old stone chimney, the only thing that remains of a ranger cabin that used to rest here. Those ruins have become a touchstone of sorts for hikers who venture to this summit. Now, Janelle walks there alone and lays her hand on the cold surface of the chimney before turning to us, her quest complete.

I walk over and we share a loud high five, and before Alex and Sage can join us I lean over and say, "I'm proud of you."

And like that, we're done. Over the course of 371 days, Janelle and I have hiked more than 225 miles. As the girls giggle and share snacks, Steve and Trish both give me a hug and I'm able to enjoy this moment for myself a bit.

"She's so strong," Trish says.

And I know what Trish means. Janelle is strong, physically, but then most kids are and can be. But there's a different sort of strength needed for a 10-year-old to do what Tough Cookie has done, a strength of character that is often overlooked when we think of children.

We still have a ridge hike ahead of us, since 4,006-foot Mt. Waumbek is less than a mile away. We still have to return safely, of course. And we have family waiting to help us celebrate. But she has everything ahead of her, anything she wishes, anything she wants to become.

I watch her play with her two friends in the snow, here above the clouds, and she glances in my direction and catches my eye, and winks.

At that moment, the potential of the universe expands before me and I understand how much I have as well.

Mt. Starr King   *November 11, 2012*

SUMMIT ELEVATION 3,907 feet

LOCATION AND DIRECTIONS Jefferson. The trailhead and parking are on gravel Starr King Road, which leaves from the north side of Route 2 in Jefferson 0.2 mi. east of its junction with Route 115A. Follow Starr King Road for about a quarter mile to a small parking area on the right.

OUR ROUTE Starr King Trail, up and back, including side trip to Mt. Waumbek.

TRIP MILEAGE 7.2 miles.

IF YOU GO If Starr King is your only destination, the round trip is 5.4 miles. It's rare for a hiker to tackle this summit without also continuing on to Mt. Waumbek, an easy walk up the ridge. *Warning:* During winter, Mt. Starr King Road may not be accessible. In that case, you'll need to park in the lot for the Jefferson village swimming pool along Route 2 near the Route 2–115A intersection, and walk the road to the trailhead.

EPILOGUE

The End, the Beginning

Waumbek is a whisper.

Upon reaching her first 4,000-footer, after this past year of triumphs, open spaces and spectacular landscapes, Janelle stands for a moment at the viewless summit looking at the snowy cairn marking the top. Her friends Alex and Sage are already settling in, digging into their packs for snacks. They've reached many such summits before and are familiar with the satisfaction of a below tree-line goal.

Janelle is not.

"Congrats, kid-o," I say, "you're now 6 feet over 4,000 feet, the highest you've ever been."

She wants to ask me where the heck is the view? Later, she will timidly ask just how many 4,000 footers are below treeline. Instead, for now, she smiles and says, "Thanks!" The joy of the 52 With a View list is that every reward, on every hike, is external. There is some view, somewhere, waiting on every hike.

The 4,000-footer list? Well, let's just say you have to find inner peace on some of those hikes. That's another lesson for another time. And in the end, I don't even know if Janelle is interested in pursuing the 4,000-footers. I suspect she'll hike with me wherever I take her, but just as our quest for the 52 was a mutual project, I want our next "list" to be mutual as well.

So, for now, the girls celebrate Janelle's accomplishment with candy bars and cookies. And we all head down the trail a ways and do find a nice view near the summit. Gray Jays buzz above our heads, little blurs. For some reason, they do not land on our hands today. That's a joy that will have to wait for Janelle.

The others leave us at this lookout, and I have a few moments to watch the girl as she tries to attract the birds, standing there atop her

Tough Cookie begins another list, New Hampshire's 4,000-footers,
by tagging Mount Waumbek.

highest mountain, all 52 (plus 1) peaks behind us. I try to be in the now, but I fail. The future is calling.

"Ready to go?" I ask.

She takes a deep breath, wipes her gloved hands and turns away from the view. "Yeah."

LATER, as we pull up the road leading to the cabin, we spot Aaron. He sees us and tears back up the road toward the cabin.

"Was that Aaron?" Janelle asks.

"I think they might be planning something," Steve says from the back.

We park and Janelle runs back to Alex and Sage's car and the three girls stroll into the cabin together. There, friends and family await, and cheers of "Surprise!" and "Congratulations!" echo through the woods. There's pizza, and ice cream and a beautiful cake, built by Meena and topped with a spectacular Marzipan hiker Janelle that Tough Cookie's aunt Nancy from Ohio created and mailed to us days earlier.

The walls are decorated with pictures of Janelle from our hikes.

And the evening passes joyfully. Janelle tells stories about her mountains, about her sore feet, the long days, eating too much peanut butter and jelly and hiking in the dark.

I watch from a distance; today is her day. Today the world itself is hers. I catch her eye now and again looking for, I don't know, regret that this chapter is done? But she's surrounded by friends and there are no more miles for her to hike, unless she wants to.

SINCE THAT victorious day, we have hiked without order or demand. We've started a new theme, urban hiking. We love visiting parks in cities, and the girl likes nothing more than to explore an old ruin in the woods. So we've stayed local, seeking out obscure trails and preservation lands far from the tourist paths.

One excursion back to the Whites fulfilled a promise I made to her on the trail, to hike across a frozen lake and visit an Appalachian Mountain Club hut. We chose Lonesome Lake in Franconia Notch, and on a beautiful February day we snowshoed across the lake and spent the afternoon exploring the warm, comfortable hut.

We sat together at the table, sipping tea and soup, devouring cheese slices and granola. The warm sun streamed through the big windows, and I watched Janelle watch the hut master, an energetic young woman with a ski hat and large, blue sunglasses.

After a moment, Janelle asked softly, "How old do you have to be to work here?"

She wants to continue, my mountain partner. She wants to hike 4,000-footers and she wants to research a new list, created by Sage and Alex called the Terrifying 25. It's a list of 25 of the most difficult trails in the Whites, so difficult in fact that even the list's creators won't be hiking some of them for a few more years.

Tough Cookie swears that she won't abandon me, that I will always be her partner.

"Even when you're old enough to hike with your own friends?" I asked.

"Of course!" she said.

"Even when you decide to hike the AT?"

"Sure, you'll be retired and we can do it together."

"Even when you learn how to scale cliffs and rock climb?"

She paused. "Well..."

But really, even if she decides to hang up her hiking boots, it wouldn't matter. Her and I have had a glorious opportunity given to few, taken advantage of by even fewer.

We taught each other how to walk farther, need less, be in the moment and stop, literally, to smell the roses, or at least smell the moose scat.

Our adventures will continue, I'm certain. But where? And how? That's up to her.

ACKNOWLEDGMENTS

Janelle and I hiked. But without the support of family, friends and fans, none of this would be possible. I am grateful beyond words to the many, many people who stepped up and helped.

Janelle, my spider monkey, my Dorothy, my Alice. This has been an amazing, life-changing journey. There is nothing you can't do, not a soul can hold you back from being anything you wish. Thank you for being a kind and decent sister to your brother, Aaron. You are my muse and I cannot wait to see what you inspire next.

Aaron, my buddy, Captain Chaos. Your support for us during this project was heroic, your calm patience truly a blessing. If Janelle and I were the legs of this quest, you were our heart and we could not have achieved what we did without you. Thank you for holding down the fort, and on those days when we returned dirty and exhausted, for always welcoming us home. You are my little man.

To Trish Herr, who somehow found the time to write the kind foreword to this book, and whose adventures with her amazing kids, Alex and Sage, have been an inspiration to Janelle. Thanks for being an example of what's possible.

To my editor, Lisa Parsons, and publisher, Mike Dickerman of Bondcliff Books, for seeing the potential and making it better.

To Peter Noonan, who designed the book jacket and who never complained about the early morning emails or endless tweaks and suggestions.

To my brother and friend, Jeff DeRego, for constantly leading by example. And to his kids, Ian and Meg, whom I love for their strength and humor. And to Cindy. I wish you had been here to help me celebrate, sister. It's all smaller without you.

My family has put up with me for a long time. Thank you Dad, Andrea, John, Ben, Max, Kiran, Rita and Sandeep. Thanks Mom.

To Janelle's family, who have honored me with a precious trust. You know who you are. And to Sara and Jim, for all your hard work.

To Teresa Robinson, for being an example to Janelle, and her friend.

The hiker world is full of beautiful, deeply engaged characters. Many of them took the time to hike or support us. Thanks Donna, Elizabeth, Hugh, Jeff R., Mark, Michael, Natalie, Neil, Patti and Steve. Thanks to Steve Smith for creating The Mountain Wanderer Map and Book Store, the center of the New Hampshire hiking universe, and thanks to the online hiking communities at Views from the Top, Rocks on Top, and Hike–NH. Thanks also to the Mt. Washington Observatory and everybody else who offered advice and trail intel when we needed it most. And thanks to the Over the Hill Hikers who had the audacity to create such an amazing list.

Thank you Jim Gagne, my mentor.

And finally to Meenakshi, for patience and advice, for understanding and support, and for knocking me around when I badly needed it. My rock, without you I would be cast adrift.

THE "52 WITH A VIEW" MOUNTAIN LIST

Rank	Peak	Elev-Ft	Region	Date Climbed
1	Sandwich Dome	3960	Waterville Valley	_____
2	Mt. Webster	3910	Presidential Range	_____
3	The Horn	3905	North Country	_____
4	Mt. Starr King	3898	North Country	_____
5	Shelburne Moriah	3735	Carter-Moriah Range	_____
6	Sugarloaf Mtn.	3700	Nash Stream	_____
7	North Baldface	3600	Baldface Range	_____
8	Mt. Success	3565	Mahoosuc Range	_____
9	South Baldface	3560	Baldface Range	_____
10	Mt. Chocorua	3480	Sandwich Range	_____
11	Stairs Mountain	3468	Crawford Notch	_____
12	Jennings Peak	3440	Waterville Valley	_____
13	Mt. Avalon	3440	Crawford Notch	_____
14	North Percy	3420	Nash Stream	_____
15	Mt. Resolution	3415	Crawford Notch	_____
16	Magalloway Mtn.	3383	North Country	_____
17	Mt. Tremont	3371	Crawford Notch	_____
18	Middle Sister	3354	Sandwich Range	_____
19	Kearsarge North	3268	North Conway	_____
20	Cherry Mtn.	3248	Presidential Range	_____
21	Smarts Mtn.	3238	Upper Conn. River Valley	_____
22	West Royce Mtn.	3200	Baldface Range	_____
23	Mount Paugus	3198	Sandwich Range	_____
24	North Moat Mtn.	3196	North Conway	_____
25	Imp Face	3165	Pinkham Notch	_____

Rank	Peak	Elev-Ft	Region	Date Climbed
26	Grand Monadnock	3150	Monadnock Region	_____
27	Mt. Cardigan	3123	Central New Hampshire	_____
28	Mt. Crawford	3119	Crawford Notch	_____
29	North Doublehead	3053	Jackson-Bartlett	_____
30	Mt. Parker	3004	Presidential Range	_____
31	Mt. Shaw	2990	Ossipee Range	_____
32	Eastman Mtn.	2939	Baldface Range	_____
33	Mt. Kearsarge	2920	Southern New Hampshire	_____
34	Hibbard Mtn.	2920	Sandwich Range	_____
35	Mt. Cube	2909	Connecticut River Valley	_____
36	Mt. Willard	2865	Crawford Notch	_____
37	Stinson Mountain	2840	Mount Moosilauke	_____
38	Black Mtn. (Benton)	2820	Mount Moosilauke	_____
39	Eagle Crag	2782	Baldface Range	_____
40	South Moat	2760	North Conway	_____
41	Black Mtn. (Jackson)	2757	Jackson-Bartlett	_____
42	Welch/Dickey Mtns.	2734	Waterville Valley	_____
43	Iron Mountain	2726	Jackson-Bartlett	_____
44	Mt. Potash	2680	Sandwich Range	_____
45	Blueberry Mtn.	2662	Mount Moosilauke	_____
46	Mt. Israel	2620	Squam Range	_____
47	Square Ledge	2600	Sandwich Range	_____
48	Mt. Roberts	2582	Ossipee Mountains	_____
49	Mt. Pemigewasset	2557	Franconia Notch	_____
50	Mt. Hayes	2555	Mahoosuc Range	_____
51	Middle Sugarloaf	2539	Little River Mountains	_____
52	Mt. Hedgehog	2532	Sandwich Range	_____

ABOUT THE AUTHOR

Dan Szczesny is the associate publisher of *The Hippo*, New Hampshire's largest weekly newspaper, based in Manchester. He came to the Granite State via a number of news departments from Buffalo to Philadelphia to New Jersey. An avid New England hiker and member of the Appalachian Mountain Club's White Mountains 4,000-Footer Club, Dan was married atop Mount Lafayette. He also traveled to Nepal and trekked to Everest Base Camp. Excerpts from his travelogue of the journey, "The Nepal Chronicles," can be found online at www.nepalchronicles.wordpress.com

The ongoing adventures of Buffalo and Tough Cookie can be found at www.52withaview.com

Dan lives in Manchester with his wife, Meenakshi.